Equality Now Project

Words of Advocacy, Injustice, and Celebration of Identities By HSED Students from Literacy Services of Wisconsin

Collected by Kathrine Yets

ISBN: 979-8-9855031-6-6
Printed, bound, and distributed by IngramSpark

Cover and interior design by Emily Heling

Book design, editorial, and proofreading services provided by Hard-Penned Press
an imprint of The Teaching Press at UW-Green Bay
2420 Nicolet Drive, Green Bay, Wisconsin, 54311-7001
uwgb.edu/teaching-press
teachingpress@uwgb.edu

About this Book

by Kathrine Yets, Instructor
(Ms. Kathrine)

This collection, and the Equality Now Project, started off simply as bringing nonfiction texts into HSED curriculum in order to reflect advancements in high school classrooms geared towards better college and career readiness. I took this opportunity to focus on students reading voices they could identify with or voices that would help them step outside of themselves. Peripheral voices, loud and proud, deserve to stand out and be at the forefront of the literary canon in any classroom, so students can discover themselves, their classmates, or someone new in what they read. From these readings came discussions of equity, activities full of solutions, and a final project of choice.

From the first set of ENPs in spring 2023, I knew their words and ideas needed to be seen by others. Their brilliance was not meant for the silo of archived classwork, tucked away, and never to go beyond. These students deserve to be heard, not become peripheral voices. I made a promise to them; I would find a way for their essays to be published. I would find a home to house their words to share with the world.

I searched for a press to publish an anthology of their essays. After much rejection through the process of navigating, inquiring, and waiting, I was pointed to The Teaching Press at UW-Green Bay. The pitch for the *Equality Now Project* anthology was welcomed, to say the least, and I was and still am so grateful. This "labor of love" from myself and The Teaching Press is for those students and for their beliefs in active advocacy, the fight against injustice, and self-celebration to be shared and appreciated by an audience. May their words promote the fight for equality and equity for all.

A note from Ms. Kathrine

To my students,

I am so proud of each and every one of you. Keep on sharing your truths that will make change sing. Remember, you are all presents of the present. Your powerful voices belong in the conversation of equality and equity. Grateful does not begin to describe how much your choice to share your words and ideas with me feels, but still, thank you. Thank you all for being you.

Table of Contents

Advocacy: Utopian City

Injustice: Combating Bigotry

Celebration: Reflections on Identity

Advocacy: Utopian City

Jasmine Northern

Information is Power

"Racism, bigotry, or discrimination of any form cannot be tolerated and when it occurs, should not be ignored," said Mark B. Pochapin (par. 6). Racism is still a widespread issue that is embedded in all areas of society from schools, to workplaces, and even to the criminal justice system. Same family, different colors; racism is a virus too! Black residents are also overrepresented in non-deadly and deadly force actions taken by the police. Through this life experience, I learned that taking risks is always good. We must take a stand and stand for what we believe in. Information is power. Change can occur by supporting advocacy, reducing the damage, and changing white attitudes.

Advocacy is a must. Advocacy is about helping and giving a person support to have their voice heard and to understand your rights and express your views (Braveman et al. par. 3). In life, advocacy is needed to build our public support for policies pursuing fairness, justice, and equal opportunities for all nationwide. Transforming legal advocacy by shifting the focus toward racial justice, advocates by working with and for communities of color, which have a unique opportunity to play a critical role in advancing race equity. Effective antipoverty advocacy must not only address people's basic needs, but also advance equitable opportunity and build movement toward systemic change. Structural racism leads to striking disparities in access to health care, housing, education, and employment for people of color. Let's stand for what we believe in and fight for what's right.

We need to reduce damage. "Change will not come if we wait for some other person or some other time. We are the ones we've been waiting for. We are the change that we seek," said Barack Obama. There can be no reconciliation or healing without truth. "Reducing the damage: some interventions would repair or reduce the damage that systemic racism has caused." We as one need the "'truth and reconciliation' . . . [about] the horrible truth of slavery, White supremacy, and historical and ongoing violations of rights [which] must be told and heard nationwide" (Braveman par. 30). We must include teaching about racism, and it must be overcome in this society. Repairing and reducing the damage caused by systemic racism will not eliminate it, but reparations are an important aspect of pursuing justice for all; we must let our voices be heard. Racism is a public health crisis, let's focus on our values instead of our fears, accepting the past but fighting for the future is a must.

Change must occur with white attitudes. Now when it comes to saying white, black, and color, at the end of the day we are all one. We bleed the same, so why do we have to be labeled different? To create an equal society, we must commit to making unbiased choices and being anti-racist in all aspects of our lives. In a society that privileges white people and whiteness, racist ideas are considered normal throughout our media, culture, social systems, and institutions. We can be led to believe that racism is only about an individual's mindset and actions, yet racist policies also contribute to our polarization. White individual's choices are damaging. Racist ideas in policy have a wide-spread impact by threatening equity of our systems and the fairness of our institutions. Awareness should include understanding by white people of how they have benefited from systemic racism and what they have to gain from living in a more just society. "In this country, American means white. Everybody else has to hyphenate," said Toni Morrison ("Whiteness" par. 7).

We must take a stand and stand for what we believe in. Information is power. Change can occur by supporting advocacy, reducing the damage, and changing white attitudes. "For those of us who work to raise the racial consciousness of whites, simply getting whites to acknowledge that our race gives us advantages is a major effort. The defensiveness, denial, and resistance are deep," said Robin DiAngelo ("Whiteness" par. 20). If we take the time to see things, different changes can occur. We must stand for what's right and overcome racism. Stick together as one and use words of power to change lives and beliefs.

Works Cited

Braveman, Paula A., et al. "Systemic And Structural Racism: Definitions, Examples, Health Damages, And Approaches to Dismantling." *Health Affairs*, vol. 41, no. 2, Feb. 2022, www.healthaffairs.org/doi/10.1377/hlthaff.2021.01394, Accessed 16 April 2023.

Pochapin, Mark B. "ACG: Racism, Bigotry, Discrimination of any Form Cannot be Tolerated, Ignored." *Healio Gastroenterology*, 2 June 2020, www.healio. com/news/gastroenterology/20200602/acg-racism-bigotry-discrimination-of-any-form-cannot-be-tolerated-ignored.

"Whiteness." *National Museum of African American History and Culture*. 19 Sept. 2022, nmaahc.si.edu/learn/talking-about-race/topics/whiteness, Accessed 16 April 2023.

La Soupe and Soup Kitchens

The painting right above us has no real painter's content behind it. Those who know Pablo Picasso's work, you are right this is one of them. It has a title behind it, named *The Soup* or *La Soupe*. This is my first time looking at one of his famous paintings. I have read some info from The Art Institute of Chicago. So really I will describe this piece of art according to my point of view, it is not intended to offend anyone.

As I've read from The Art Institute of Chicago, this piece was one of his Blue Periods, just like that they capitalize it. I took a longer look and sure, he does have other paintings that are blue, mostly the background looks dark like if the moon has come down on his setting. If I had a question for him it would be: did you roleplay this image or is it something you've seen during your time? Well, this painting looks beautiful and its color blue is also a color of tranquility (calm).

The night has set everyone in their gowns, but it did throw me off a bit when I read something from "The Soup, 1902 by Pablo Picasso." The question was, "Is the older woman physically weighed down by her destitution, giving the soup to the small child or receiving it from her?" (par. 2). There I say, this is where your heart counts. The child looks like she is rushing to receive the soup, but also her hand fades as if she just handed the older woman the soup. Before I get to another point of view, what education are we at with each other — is there a perfect stance for handing someone something? Now the receiver has her hip out as if she was patiently waiting for the child to receive. What is your thought on that hip? Have you ever been in a place quite like this: quiet open range, no city lights? I personally think she's making sure the young one doesn't go to sleep hungry, a little bit of soup will do it. They also mention Picasso was surrounded by poverty ("Pablo Picasso: Paintings, Bios & Quotes" par. 9). Surely she was an overworking woman and might have been just grateful to even have soup to provide for the child. Usually, nights like this are a bit chilly wouldn't you agree?

It's a beautiful painting. I'm not one hundred percent sure what this painting meant to him or meant to show the world. Would we have the same point of view if age differs? What would be new generations' thoughts of it? "Picasso centers the act of charity upon the basic need for nourishment" ("The Soup, 1902" par. 2). Well if he did not write it himself or leave it in a specific hand to explain it, I could not tell you. Every bit of research helps and gives clues.

Have you ever stayed out too late and the doors were locked at a certain time? Now you would be out for the night. You'd be lucky if someone had left an open bag of Cheetos on the porch that evening. Well luckily for me a friend adopted me. He is around the same age, I would say. We did not have much luck at the time with finding a job, not sure for a couple of years. I'll say the city was overpopulated. What I really want to add is someone was always cooking and inviting with a plate.

What kind of a person are you when seeing someone in need? Lucky for some, there are soup kitchens. I've done some community service in my younger days. You should try it. Living in the city, my mother used to buy a couple bags of chicken legs and fry 'em up for the kids around the block and for us, not asking for a cent. How do we live with ourselves just chasing money? Are we being generous? Poverty does have its millions of questions before an actual result and answer we can say.

What we can do is lend a hand. Not only donate money but time. Share who you are and your skills. Be kind, generous, and happy. No matter the challenges that we come across there will always be someone in that kitchen if that someone isn't you already. Food drives: we thank you.

Works Cited

"Pablo Picasso: 150 Famous Paintings, Bio & Quotes by Picasso." *PabloPicasso.org*, www.pablopicasso.org/.

"Pablo Picasso." *The Art Institute of Chicago*, www.artic.edu/artists/36198/pablo-picasso.

"The Soup, 1902 by Pablo Picasso." *PabloPicasso.org*, www.pablopicasso.org/the-soup.jsp#.

Kathryn Yang

Paying It Forward

"For the first time in my life, someone actually listened to me" words of a survivor about their experience with CRAY ("For Youth" slide 6). Pre-teens don't want to live with their parents anymore, while their minds pull their souls into this world of trouble. Sometimes being a pre-teen and into a teenager our lives are different, some may be by themselves. For unstable children, usually family is the cause of it. Therefore, families that are in need and have nowhere to stay, I have resources for you as well! For those who need help out here, I suggest you stop by Pathfinders, Walker's Point, and finally, The Cathedral Center, Inc.

Over the last 52 years, Pathfinders has been the most empowering and engaging with youth that are in need. Pathfinders not only have a drop-in center, but they also have a shelter that has gradually continued growing. Their drop-in center has lots of resources itself. They accept the ages from 11-25. The drop-in has showers, hygiene products, free laundry services, computer labs, helps people find housing, and is a safe, comfortable place to just hang out and chill. They have a therapist and, most recently, a place where mandated and non-mandated reporters are available. When you age out, don't worry, Pathfinders won't let you go like that! They help you find resources that are acceptable for your needs. Their shelter allows the ages from 11-17 where if you are a runaway or homeless, they help you! You can stay there for up to two weeks. Within those weeks, time will fly and you will definitely be fulfilled with their service. However, Pathfinders is not the only safe place, there is Walker's Point as well.

Walker's Point has been a safe environment for youths from ages 11-17. You can call them and explain your situation that you're homeless and they will help you find your way to them. They may not have the same options as Pathfinders, but Walker's Point has been here for more than 50 years. They have counseling in which you can go by appointment or walk in. Their primary goal is to reunite the youth with their families to resolve their issues. You can stay up to 21 days at their emergency shelter. During your stay, you're going to accomplish lots, but only if you participate. Though it's hard to do counseling with your family, it's an opportunity to grow from the negativity so that together they can go home safely and comfortably. Though you do have your own counseling sessions, you can use that time to express anything you are feeling to overcome it yourself or with your counselor. If you're in the distance of home and school during your stay, they provide you with bus fare and if you don't know how to take the bus, they are open to go with you so you are comfortable. Although this is a great resource: families, single mothers, single fathers, or two-parent households, you're in luck, I welcome you to the Cathedral Center!

Call 211! There are more resources when you call it, but specifically, the Cathedral Center (CCI) helps out families. Being unemployed with children, they can help watch your children if you want them to, just so you can get back onto your feet. They give you the best opportunity to choose the right path for you and your family. CCI began as a community-wide collaboration for the shelters, specifically for women and children. Other shelters that they partnered up with are the American Red Cross, Interfaith Conference of Greater Milwaukee, Columbia St. Mary's, St. Ben's Clinic (now Ascension St. Ben's Clinic), Milwaukee County Department of Health & Human Services, Catholic Charities of the Archdiocese of Milwaukee, Inc., and Cathedral of St. John the Evangelist. These are other shelters that involve families in need. CCI not only opens up to single women and children, but single men with children. Though its focus is for women, they opened up their arms to see both genders and know that there aren't many resources for single men. These places, when you get there may be a little bit alarming, but it's a safe place and you have a roof over you and your family's heads. It's just a push to help you get back onto your feet. These are resources I've gathered in this world filled with imperfection. With more of these resources, we could help one another out, in a tough situation.

Gathering Pathfinders, Walker's Point, and Cathedral Center and making it five times bigger would be the world's number one world record to stop the homelessness of a youth or a family that wasn't mentally prepared. Everyone isn't educated the same way. Many have levels of ups and downs. The fact that many youths run away because of family situations means things tend to be unsolved and a youth is just learning how this world is. Then comes the family part, of when the parents themselves aren't stable, not knowing the aftermath. Is there support? Are you alone? I am a survivor with no parental support. Hear me out as these resources I've used to help me, can also help you.

Works Cited

Cathedral Center. cathedral-center.org/.

"For Youth." *CRAY: Collaborative Rapid Advocacy for Youth*, craymke.org/for-youth/.

Pathfinders. www.pathfindersmke.org/.

Walker's Point: Youth and Family Center. www.walkerspoint.org/.

Utopia

Why? Why? Why is there so much trash everywhere you turn? I know I'm tired of all the trash in the streets. Everyday I come outside it encourages me to do something. This is a reason why we have to stand together within everything. We have a great opportunity coming up in the summer, but this doesn't have to be a summer opportunity. You can make this a career. New Milwaukee is on the rise. With this opportunity, you can be hands-on with your children, you will have a great support system, and you will even get some positive impact. When you join this family, everyone will enjoy it and also get money while doing it. We can make this city strong again with New Milwaukee in partnership with Heal the Hood, Our Next Generation, and Mr. Bob's Under the Bridge.

Every weekend you will be able to explore the different neighborhoods in Milwaukee. Heal the Hood is partnering up with me. We will be hosting block parties in these neighborhoods. While hosting them, we will provide entertainment, food, and games all while cleaning up our areas — building and bringing neighborhoods together as a union bonding a community. We can take care of the community as a team with families.

Many families may need a support team to build a strong and firm family. Our Next Generation is here to assist also. Our Next Generation can help build a collaborative network of parents and families, while "expanding students' horizons by exposing them to a variety of enriching environments and potential future careers," giving everyone the tools they may need. As well as investing students in "protecting, improving, and taking pride in their neighborhood and local community" ("Who We Are" par. 3).

When you take pride in something, you give back, that's where Mr. Bob's Under the Bridge comes in. Mr. Bob's Under the Bridge is the last organization to help assist in expanding the love throughout the community. We will go throughout Milwaukee feeding the homeless hot meals and leaving them with a cold lunch bag for later. We will do outreach. Items such as clothes, hygiene kits, and snacks are distributed at each location with our four-stall shower trailer also following to offer a safe place to bathe if needed.

It's not hard building and making things strong again when you have a team. When everyone is focused on the same thing, you can achieve. With Heal the Hood spreading entertainment and cleaning, Our Next Generation giving the tools to help build a support team, and Mr. Bob's Under the Bridge giving back, they show a positive impact towards making this a new city.

New Milwaukee is going to be huge, not leaving a community behind. So come help in this family impact.

Works Cited

Heal The Hood. healthehoodmke.org, Accessed 26 April 2023.

Mr. Bob's Under the Bridge. mrbobsunderthebridge.org/, Accessed 26 April 2023.

"Who We Are." *Our Next Generation*. www.ongkids.org/about, Accessed 26 April 2023.

Milwaukee Organizations for the People

The reason I chose these three organizations is because I can relate to them. Big Brothers, Big Sisters addresses youths in America and helps them make better decisions. Sojourner gives you all the resources you need coming out of a domestic violence relationship. Milwaukee Habitat for Humanity gives you the opportunity to become a homeowner. My parents donate to Sojourner. Every few months they have inspired me to do the same.

Big Brothers, Big Sisters brings change to my area in so many ways. Most children are believed to be a product of their environment. I live in the 53206 ZIP Code where I've seen so many bad things happen. In fact, it is said to be one of the worst ZIP Codes in Wisconsin, and some children and teens tend to navigate towards the negativity they are surrounded by. We have a very bad epidemic: stolen vehicles, along with reckless driving, killing, or badly injuring our youth. The people in the Big Brothers, Big Sisters program give our teens hope and a better chance at success, with hundreds of children needing a caring adult role model. They are more likely to avoid the bad influences around them with this program. I believe it will create change in the world, in our children, and in the community we live in.

Sojourner helps our community in countless ways by addressing domestic violence prevention and intervention. This nonprofit organization is close to home with me because I am a survivor of domestic violence and didn't know where to turn after running away from my abuser. I found the Sojourner Truth House. They changed my life in numerous ways, offering me a warm place to sleep, a safe place to be, and food to eat. Sojourner helps with restraining orders, housing, and job help. "The economic losses, arising directly from injury and loss of life resulting from intimate partner violence is $82.3 million and the economic loss is $113.1 million annually in Milwaukee County alone" (Von Nessen et al. par. 2). I believe this organization helps build up the women in our community every day.

Milwaukee Habitat for Humanity is building the community and making it possible to be a homeowner. "One in three Milwaukee renters spend half or more than half of their income on housing" ("Housing Affordability" par. 2). With the Habitat for Humanity organization, you get help with different housing choices. They also help fix your credit and give you options to help with a down payment. They build new homes in the communities we live in, and they also rehab houses that have been abandoned or foreclosed. This program helps our community with limiting the amount of abandoned houses that we have. I believe this organization to be a great stepping stone to home ownership.

In closing, I believe the three organizations listed are changing my community one day at a time. With caring people helping other people, the passion seen in these places lets you know that there are still some good people in the world. The education alone that these people bring is amazing. I believe these organizations will continue to help the community many years from now.

Works Cited

Big Brothers Big Sisters of America. 2019, www.bbbs.org/.

"Housing Affordability." *Milwaukee Habitat for Humanity*, milwaukeehabitat.org/about/housing-affordability/#:⬚:text=1%20in%203%20Milwaukee%20renters,-decent%20and%20affordable%20housing%20provides.

Milwaukee Habitat for Humanity. 2024, milwaukeehabitat.org/.

Sojourner. www.familypeacecenter.org/.

Von Nessen, Joseph C. and Erin Schubert. "The Economic Impact of Domestic Violence In Milwaukee & Wisconsin 2021." *Sojourner & Jamie Kimble Foundation For Courage*, Oct. 2022, static1.squarespace.com/static/5d39f654dfc553000198b222/t/6345b7f7fc2276703a2bf19d/1665513464758/Economic+Impact+of+DV+FINAL.+10.11.2022.pdf.

Rosemary Bostwick

The Brothertown Indian

Did you know that my family descends from the Brothertown Indians? The Brothertown Indians believed that continuity, survival, and autonomy were important. During the start of the Brothertown Indians, they had issues with land and were forced to move and make their land smaller. Today the Brothertown Indians live across the Midwest. They have approximately 4,000 members ("Brothertown Indians" par. 4). Overall, the Brothertown Indians are a tribe that helps its members achieve the best version of themselves, build a strong community, and preserve their culture and history.

Firstly, the Brothertown Indians help members become the best version of themselves. They hold regional events to practice culture and community. The Brothertown Indians hold powwows to educate others about community and heritage. Brothertown Indians believe in spreading Christianity to Indigenous communities. They envisioned the new community as governed in a manner that combined tribal and democratic systems of government.

Secondly, the Brothertown Indians built a strong community. The Brothertown Indians came from New England and the eastern parts of Long Island. They moved out west so they could live in peace away from European American influences. Upon arrival, the Brothertown Indians built a church, cleared their communal land, and began farming. They built sawmills, grist mills, and tanneries. The Brothertown Indians had their land reduced because many other Indians moved in and then by state action, the Brothertown Indians were pressured to sell or lease their land (Loew par. 2).

Thirdly, the Brothertown Indians preserve their culture and history. The goal of the Brothertown Indians is to bring back and protect their unique historical, cultural, and traditional beliefs. Keeping their history and culture safe is important so as to keep them from being forgotten. They also try to preserve their way of life and promote positive images of everyone that include honesty, integrity, and fairness. Overall, the Brothertown Indians try to keep their history and culture from dissipating and promote positive self-images.

Finally, the Brothertown Indian Nation is one of 12 tribes that reside in Wisconsin ("About Our Heritage" par. 2), but is the only one that isn't federally recognized. The Brothertown Indian Nation continues its long-standing effort to regain its federal recognition. Overall, the Brothertown Indians hit many obstacles from moving, to losing land, and fighting to be recognized. To this day they are still fighting to be a recognized tribe. Recognize the Brothertown Indians and make efforts to help them be recognized federally.

In conclusion, the Brothertown Indians are a tribe that believe that community and self-fulfillment are very important. They help everyone in the tribe build good values and become determined in what they want in life. They also have built a strong community while dealing with many issues with land and the government, but still persevering through all of it. Finally, they try to keep their history and culture safe so they don't lose sight of what's important in life. Therefore, the Brothertown Indians believe that building a strong community and having good values are very important and never try to lose sight of that.

Works Cited

"About Our Heritage and Culture." *Brothertown Indian Nation*, brothertownindians.org/.

"Brothertown Indians." *Wikipedia*, en.wikipedia.org/wiki/BrothertownIndians.

Loew, Patty. "The Brothertown Indian Nation: A Brief Introduction." *Wisconsin Historical Society*, www.wisconsinhistory.org/Records/Article/CS4358.

Injustice: Combating Bigotry

Enid Ortiz

Sexism and Its Effects

Does sexism affect the way we watch television today? Consider the way others suggest that members of the opposite sex are less able than the other or just refer to the other sex's bodies, behavior, and feelings in a negative way for everyone to see. The sexism we see on TV and in our everyday life has been going on for a long time. Especially in how they advertise sexism for marketers to meet their sales and downgrading the opposite sex. Sexism is prevalent on television as far as doxa, gender, and age.

In the article "Gender and Age Inequalities in Television and News Production Culture in Poland: Ethnography in a Public Broadcasting Company" by Greta Gober, it explains, "The Television game has its own rules, logic, and dominant practices, known as the doxa" (53). The meaning of doxa, according to Wikipedia, is "to appear, to seem, to think, to accept . . . a popular opinion" ("Doxa" par. 2), which is what the media does on television today, just all a part of their game. There is age discrimination between both sexes. It's okay for an older man to play a larger role on TV, but not for older women; they get the smaller roles. This was mentioned in an interview with Michal, a manager of 13 years with public broadcasting company Telewizja Polska (TVP), simply because women don't want to show themselves anymore due to their age (Gober 56-57). It shows how strongly they cater to their ratings from the audience and how that can establish such behavior. This proves how racism and sexism are being advertised on television; they discriminate against women for ratings and money. As a woman, I feel hurt and disgusted at how they portray us because of our gender.

Women are always being discriminated against on television as far as how the perspective of a woman is supposed to look and be like. Women start to lose focus on themselves and go through cosmetic surgery just to be able to fit the part. According to an interview with Kamila from TVP, she exemplifies that women have to be beautiful on television because it's much nicer to look at pretty ladies (Gober 57-58). "Kamila worked for a commercial television station in Poland for 20 years before she joined TVP" (Gober 58). This also proves the image women have to keep up with in order to be on television and how doxa plays a big role in sexism for women in general.

I believe that sexism does affect the way we watch television today because of everything they play on it. As a woman and a single mother of two girls, I'm scared for them to grow up in this world.

There's no escaping sexism in this environment we live in. It's all over the TV and shows we watch, even on the ads that advertise it like it's okay. We have to stand together as strong women and use our voices and resources to make a change.

Works Cited

"Doxa." *Wikipedia*, en.wikipedia.org/wiki/Doxa.

Gober, Greta. "Gender and Age Inequalities in Television and News Production Culture in Poland: Ethnography in a Public Broadcasting Company." *Critical Studies in Television: The International Journal of Television Studies*, vol.15, no.1, pp. 49-68, Sage Journals, 18 March 2020, doi.org/10.1177/1749602019891542.

Vincente Rodriguez

Sexism in Wrestling

Sexism is still very present in 2024. Something that was practiced in the 1940s and 50s is unfortunately still very alive today. Sexism is still seen on television, social media, and more. Often, sexism is also seen in wrestling. It is something I have been watching since I can remember and still do at 26 years old. There also definitely was a lot of racism when I watched it as a child that I never realized was racism until my later teens. There has been so much change but still very similar patterns. Sexism is still active in the wrestling industry, but changes have been made since the company has grown.

The male and female gaze is apparent within wrestling. When most think of wrestling, they think of men. One big wrestling company is a company named World Wrestling Entertainment (WWE). It was created in 1953, with mostly men being the center of the company. As the years went on, women only came out to accompany many of the male wrestlers, and wore minimal clothing. Many of the women wore revealing lingerie, bras/panties, and more. Women would come out beside a male wrestler as an accessory and not a wrestler. They came out to make the men look good. The women were not seen as wrestlers due to their physicality and appearance. "In 2008, WWE entered its PG Era and adapted a family-friendly format. WWE distanced itself from the sexual content that was pervasive throughout previous eras. However, the role of women within WWE during this time was criticized because their matches were not as integral to the show as male wrestler's matches were" ("Women in WWE" par. 24).

Once women began wrestling, more and more women came out to be wrestlers. They still, however, did not treat them too fairly within this realm. As they allowed them to dress in their own ways, they still controlled how often the women were televised and allowed to fight. As the years went on, WWE continued to have more female talent represent the company, but it was still kept to a minimum. In the early years, many of the women only had one match a week and it was the designated one that was picked by management. When it came to fights, the show was hosted two days a week, Mondays and Fridays. Between those two days, there were at most three out of 12 fights that consisted of just women. Based on some statistics, as of July 2023 there were, "55 matches involving women so far, compared to the 136 matches involving men. The average length of a women's match on RAW is 7:22 minutes, compared to the 9:09 minutes of the men. The women have 24.58% of wrestling time for themselves, while the men have the remaining 75.42%" (@thelumpur par. 21).

Nowadays wrestling has evolved to be very inclusive, with female wrestlers and many wrestlers of different ethnic backgrounds. Now in 2024, women are one of the biggest parts of the company. In previous years and eras, WWE defined the women as "Divas," and named a title after them, "WWE Divas Championship." "At WrestleMania 32 in 2016, WWE announced their discontinuation of the "Diva" branding for its female performers, as part of a move to present them in an athletic manner more in line with their male counterparts, rather than in a means based around sex appeal" ("Women in WWE" par. 2). Now in 2024, there are multiple champions in the company that are women and they are amazing. The women are allowed to do what they desire and don't need to dress a certain way to appease the fans or management. Some of the biggest female wrestlers have even gotten the chance to headline a premium live event. They have become the company, and they have become a huge face of the WWE. There have been many female wrestlers from different cultural backgrounds and races who have become champions: African American, Irish, Australian, Caucasian, and many more. The women come out in all different types of attire, while some are revealing, some aren't. But it is based on the wrestler's choice, and what they want to do. "Women's wrestling has made a splash in media and entertainment, showing how much it's grown and changed. There was a time when female wrestlers were hardly seen or talked about in the media, but now, they're everywhere! They're treated just like the men, as equals, and they get as much attention for their fights and stories. This big change has helped more people see women's wrestling in a new light, making it more popular and respected than ever before" ("Cultural Impact of Women's Wrestling" par. 11).

Sexism has changed, but has not at the same time. It has gotten better, but it is still very present in 2024. It is everywhere within social media, movies, TV shows, and other media. It's inevitable. Many people in the world still believe in gender roles, such as women only being in the kitchen and men working all the time. It's unfair. It is unrealistic to only allow men to do a certain thing, and women to do a certain thing. We should all be allowed to do what our hearts desire and make us happy. Not what society says we should do. As a male who grew up with a single mother, in a female-dominated household, I learned the value of men helping and being the support to women, and how women are capable of anything a man can do, and vice versa. I recommend anyone who wants to watch something new to watch wrestling and see how amazing a lot of the women are, and how strong and physical they can be. Also, don't be scared to try something new because you're male or female. If you want to do or try something, do it.

Don't let anybody stop you or judge you because it's a "man's job" or a "woman's job." Anyone can do anything, as long as they set their mind to it and ignore the negativity.

Works Cited

Borland, Elizabeth. "Standpoint Theory." *Encyclopaedia Britannica*, www.britannica.com/topic/standpoint-theory.

"The Cultural Impact of Women's Wrestling in America." *American Women's Wrestling*, 7 Feb. 2024, www.americanwomenswrestling.com/guest/the-cultural-impact-of-womens-wrestling-in-america.

Loreck, Janice. "Explainer: What Does the 'Male Gaze' Mean, and What About a Female Gaze?" *Monash University*, 22 Jan. 2016, www.monash.edu/news/articles/9735.

@thelumpur. "An In-Depth Analysis of the Women's Wrestling Time in WWE, AEW and Impact." *Reddit*, www.reddit.com/r/SquaredCircle/comments/15d649v/anindepthanalysisofthewomenswrestlingtime/.

"Women in WWE." *Wikipedia*, 15 Apr. 2024, en.wikipedia.org/wiki/WomeninWWE.

Luis Flores

Sexism in Military Cinema

Gender discrimination in military movies has been shown by excluding women in most of these films. Let's talk about how the media keeps sexism alive. Have you ever noticed how the media promotes the idea of equal rights for women but continues to show sexist beliefs toward them? Sexism is the reality within military cinema based on lack of representation and how they are represented.

Sexism is present from objectification and unrealistic beauty standards, to some forms of discrimination, and even excluding females in movies either partially or entirely. In an article called "Military Women in World Cinema: A 20th Century History and Filmography, Introduction" it states that, "[Women] were excluded from the films altogether or were included only as love interests, typically working in traditional roles as wives or nurses" (Deacon and Fowler 9). I am now noticing this because my wife showed interest in the US military, and I have seen many military movies that exclude women. The presence of sexist beliefs is crystal clear to this day.

As my wife developed an interest and started exploring opportunities with the US military, I couldn't help but become more observant of the representation of women in these kinds of movies. I have seen many movies from years ago to now, that have excluded women partially, if not altogether. We watched a few movies within a couple of weeks and after watching them I told my wife, "Have you noticed all these movies rarely show women?" This one movie called *American Sniper,* a true story, was the one that made me realize this. All of the soldiers were men. They even showed how the war in the Middle East was, where they would use kids to kill off soldiers. But not one of those soldiers were women. The media should show real and empowering women in all fields, including the military, to ensure that future generations are inspired by the diverse and great contributions that women make to society.

The media has serious power in shaping how we see gender roles and what's considered "normal." It has the power to either stick with old stereotypes or change things. And even though it has changed a lot, we still see a lot of the same things happening. They try to show and talk about self-love and body positivity, that they recognize beauty comes in all shapes, sizes, colors, and forms – but then, all the ads show most of the same size models. Not just for women, but men, too. When you see clothes commercials, you rarely see someone plus-sized. Even the "plus-sized" are not what one would say has a heavy build. The media must keep changing these norms and fully accept the variety of individuals. How does this connect to military cinema?

The media's opinion of women impacts real views on society. Different and empowering representations, including in male-dominated fields like the military, can inspire gender equality and empower future generations. As we continue to use the media, pay attention to the things the media shows us. We should support and promote more inclusive ways for everyone.

Works Cited

Deacon, Deborah A., and Stacy Fowler. "Military Women in World Cinema: A 20th Century History and Filmography, Introduction." *Digital Commons at Saint Mary's University,* August 2023, commons.stmarytx.edu/cgi/viewcontent.cgi?article=1712&context=facarticles.

Regina M. Scott

How the Media Has Harmed Women

Have you ever seen a woman in the media for an advertisement for clothes? She doesn't have many clothes on, let alone the clothes she's advertising.

The media thinks every woman should be without a lot of clothes on, with a lot of makeup on, and they should all be one size. That is not what I want young girls to see and think.

Advertisements have been dehumanizing women for years! I feel bad for the young ladies who see these ads and feel that's how women are supposed to look to get attention. It also makes them think this is how they need to look and act, otherwise society won't accept them. The more I look into this, women aren't the only ones who are looked upon as sex symbols, it's also men. However, women are the ones who get portrayed in the worst ways in advertisements, just because the media thinks sex sells. There should be a limit on what they can post. If it was up to me, these ads would be put on a hot plate for how a woman's image is portrayed and treated.

The media creates sexism. According to the "Sexism & Bigotry" article, "By definition the term sexism mean[s] prejudice, stereotyping, or discrimination, typically against women, on the basis of sex; in restricted job opportunities; especially, such discrimination directed against women" ("Sexism & Bigotry" par. 1). From what I've been watching and listening to, there is a lot of sexism towards women on TV shows, movies, songs, etc. I was watching a movie where a young lady lived in a marsh all alone. So the inner city guy with wealth and power thought he could take advantage of her because of how she looked. She was attractive by societal standards, but she lived in the marsh which meant he thought she was dumb and had low self-esteem. So he thought it would be a good idea to play with her feelings while he was engaged. She came to her senses and got rid of him. The moral is don't let people treat you how they want, stand up for yourself and others who can't.

I don't think the media and these advertisements should degrade women into thinking life should go as it is presented to them in magazines. The media needs to portray self-love and acceptance of shapes, sizes, and colors. After I have read about sexism and how it still to this day makes young girls and women feel they need to look a certain way or be a certain color, why can't we all just be ourselves? I think if the media sees us women empowering ourselves and not letting them tell us what to do, they would sell more magazines because everyone would see that all the models don't look alike in color, shape, or size.

The media and all its advertisements can make a change in the world if they choose not to symbolize women with all their sexism in their ads, movies, and songs. We should be aware of this in order to take positive action rather than a negative approach based on false statements about bigotry and sexism ("Sexism & Bigotry" par. 2). If you want to know more about bigotry and sexism, follow the links below.

Works Cited and Consulted

"Sexism & Bigotry." *PhDessay.com*, 8 Aug. 2018, phdessay.com/sexism-bigotry/.

"Sexism in the Media." *PhDessay.com*, 5 Oct. 2018, phdessay.com/sexism-in-the-media/.

Jason Sanchez

Social Media and the Bystanders of Hate

Do you know how much bigotry is spread within the media? Bigotry exists in so many different ways today. So much hatred lingers throughout social media that it's hard to keep track of. There are so many people being discouraged due to all the commentary coming from different angles. Homophobia is prevalent within reels on social media, and despite platform policies, not much is being done to get this hate off social media. But people are stepping up to combat this bigotry.

So many of us wonder: will there ever be a safe space for us? According to *FirstPost*, after a video went viral about a safe space for the LGBTQIA+, it received many negative and hateful comments. "Instagram did little to secure their space" (Bhattacharjee par. 1). It has created a lingering problem for the community in India. "Indrajeet Ghorpade, founder of the digital LGBTQ awareness platform, 'Yes, We Exist,'" hosted an event to help those in the community to share their coming out experience (Bhattacharjee par. 3). It was a platform to allow those to come out to their family and friends, but still feel safe. Unfortunately, just seconds within the live event taking off, it received so much backlash that it discouraged the community. Some just no longer wanted to participate in this event. While receiving those hateful comments, they never had an option to block or report those users.

Bigotry has been shown a lot lately through short clips on YouTube or reels on TikTok. Some have shown homophobia without getting any penalties on their accounts. The internet has its ways on who they want to censor and who they don't. For the slightest thing in a caption, you can get censored and possibly even blocked from using your account for a couple days. Yet you can come across videos that are showing hatred from the slightest detail to something major, and it roams around the internet without penalties. Now, some do take action and do as the policy says, while some just may not really look further into it. Then again, we don't really know how the back end works with the policies and who enforces it.

Reels today have been used in a negative way, but also have been used in a positive way. They're being used in a comedic way but also in an inspirational way. The comedic way is a great way to reel people in to watch your clips, but it's also a great way to share the importance of change and love with everyone all around the world. Some people are fighting to show others that it's okay to be around others who are different. Be confident in yourself. We're in a new era where everyone is more accepting. They believe that in order for us to create a safe community, it's as easy as deleting, blocking, unfollowing, and removing comments. According to *FirstPost*, "it is impossible to censor the mind-boggling quantity of content that's being uploaded to [all types of] platforms" (Bhattacharjee par. 29).

Bigotry exists in so many different ways today. I've come across so many different uplifting clips. No matter how many policies they have created, it's still not enough to stop the bigotry. Let's step up and let our voices be heard. Make a change by saying something.

Work Cited and Consulted

Bhattacharjee, Puja. "Where Instagram Goes Wrong When it Comes to Safeguarding the Rights of the LGBTQIA+ Community." *Firstpost*, 7 August 2021, www.firstpost.com/india/lgbtq-community-finds-homophobia-has-a-free-run-on-instagram-and-pleas-for-help-dont-really-work-9869871.html.

Jeet. "Instagram Users Plan Lynchings At LGBT Pride In India | 5 Ways To Make Instagram Safer." *Youth Ki Awaaz*, 14 June 2021, www.youthkiawaaz.com/2021/06/insta-users-plan-lynchings-of-lgbt-people-at-pride-in-india-5-tips-to-make-insta-safer/.

Otis Jackson

What Makes Headlines

"The root of western media is white supremacy and that's where implicit bias stems from," a quote from Nissa Tzun, a panelist from the latest installment of *We Need To Talk*, a seven-part series at UNLV focusing on racism and people's beliefs that permeate society. In episode three, which was called "Communication," they discussed the bias that affects newsrooms and the communities they cover. Tzun, who is originally from Hong Kong, but moved to Canada, describes how blacks are portrayed in the media as criminals or victims of police abuse and such images can prompt immigrants to avoid the black communities as well as other minority groups because of violence. Blacks and other minority groups are and have been racially profiled in the media for years, and stereotypes of all kinds have determined how foreigners feel about certain race groups.

In today's world, we are plagued by clashes and conflicts, and the media is being racially biased — for instance, with the war in Ukraine. As foreign media covers the war, journalists are being called out for the way they are reporting it back to the people. They are accused of racialized language in the way they are reporting the war. And adding more insult to injury, African migrants were turned away while trying to flee Ukraine by train, but it wasn't highly publicized. There are black countries that are at war right now and have been at war for years, leaving a lot of people displaced and countless more dead. I agree with this author when he stated that no one really cares unless white people are affected (Asare par. 2).

In December of 2021, a 23-year-old black woman was found dead in her apartment in Bridgeport, Connecticut, and her family was never notified. Her death went unnoticed until female rapper Cardi B shared the story on social media, prompting the case to go nationwide. It's true that a lot of black women who go missing or are found dead rarely get reported, compared to the white women who will gain national attention until that person is found. However, the lack of media attention for black women has started a movement called "Say Her Name," a movement that should give them the attention they need in the time of a crisis. The black, brown, and Asian communities have to govern their own in order to protect their own (Asare par. 3).

I feel bigotry will never go away, it's evolving and the bigots are getting more strategic when applying it to certain situations. People say it starts at home but behind closed doors — what is going on? What is being said? And in today's day and age, anyone can be a bigot. A white person that has experienced bigotry calls it reverse racism, and I really don't know what that means.

That just tells me you're a racist who was discriminated against — why can't it just be simply racism? Education is the key. People have to realize we are all the same no matter what color you are or what you represent.

Works Cited

Asare, Janice Gassam. "The Pervasiveness Of Racism And Bias In The Media." *Forbes*, 28 Feb. 2022, www.forbes.com/sites/janicegassam/2022/02/28/the-pervasiveness-of-racism-and-bias-in-the-media/?sh=2da4b7f.

"Unpacking How Media Influences our Views on Racism." *We Need to Talk*, University of Nevada, Las Vegas, 26 Oct. 2020, www.unlv.edu/news/article/un-packing-how-media-influences-our-views-racism.

Leticia Garcia

Learning to Accept the World

The biggest problem on today's media platforms is racism. Racism is many things: it is prejudice, discrimination, or antagonism directed toward individual races, shown by those who believe their race is better than other races. For many years, racism has existed; it has been around for a while. Social norms and whatever is trending in the media are factors that contribute to racism.

Mass media and advances in technology directly impact the issue of racism. Often times the media is what shapes society's beliefs and principles. Most racism seen over the years has been focused on African Americans, but other races do experience just as much racism, if not more. It is the media that makes society focus on racism toward African Americans specifically.

The crucial role played by the media is to make people conform to social norms. "As stated by Day (2009), racism is prejudice with power against the people of color who during this case comprise African-Americans, Hispanic, Asian Americans, and Native Americans. Day (2009) noticed that racism isn't always a conscious effort" ("Impacts of Mass Media" par. 3). The media influences society's beliefs and morals because it has become the new way for people to get their daily/current news and things that are trending.

The Windrush scandal in the UK helped to reveal just how the media demonstrates racism, both directly and indirectly. Broadcasters portray people of color in the press and it has "escalated their criticism in respect to 'a white, classed, and gendered British norm' (Edwards 2018)" ("Impacts of Mass Media" par. 4). The Windrush scandal happened when the United Kingdom government was accused of institutional racism. Institutional racism is when government institutions, school systems, and public institutes fail to protect people based on their ethnicity, culture, and religion. There needs to be specialized programs/services to support people who are different and come from different backgrounds.

Social norms will always be a direct contributor to a lot of the racism experienced today. The problem comes when minority children are raised to identify with their own race and recognize what sets them apart, but racism has caused harm to minorities because of how they are viewed in the eyes of society. It is always the bad things that are shared in the media, never anything good. This causes society to also only focus on the bad and then the bad is all that they believe that another race is capable of. "Ethnic and racial membership is an important factor in one's identity (Pauker, Apfelbaum, & Spitzer 2015)" ("Impacts of Mass Media" par. 5). Social norms continue to affect the behavior and attitudes of the younger generation. Racism has changed over the years, just as technology has. People are learning to be more accepting of new ways of life and are altering their way of viewing the world. However, there are still going to be those people who are stuck in their old ways of thinking/ living and will never change. It is up to the younger generation to raise their offspring to view themselves as equal versus superior to others.

Works Cited

"The Impacts Of Mass Media In Racism." *Edubirdie*, 18 Jul. 2021, edubirdie.com/examples/the-impacts-of-mass-media-in-racism/, Accessed 4 Dec. 2022.

Katravia Lee

The Most Powerful Entity on Earth

Did you know that bigotry in the media is still prevalent today? The great Malcolm X is quoted to have said, "the media's the most powerful entity on earth. They have the power to make the innocent guilty and to make the guilty innocent, and that's power. Because they control the minds of the masses." The fact is that it's still happening today, and something needs to be done about it so the world can be a better place. Bigotry is put into the media through movies, commercials, TV shows, and through modern media or the internet.

Bigotry is still present in the media through television shows and movies. According to the study by *The Guardian*, "television and streaming shows always ignore racial disparities in the criminal justice system" (Evelyn par. 9). "In fictional crime shows, blacks and persons of color, even when depicted as criminal justice professionals, are often shortchanged or misrepresented. The Netflix show *Luke Cage* portrays illegal acts having been committed 100% of the time by a person of color. ABC's *How to Get Away with Murder* portrays crimes by persons of color 67% of the time" (Fortino par. 7).

"In the psychological thriller, *Get Out*, writer/director Jordan Peele explores race in the context of post-racial liberalism in America. The film uncovers the attitudes of white liberals towards black people in order to reinforce this race relationship in modern times where many of these people convince themselves that they have 'moved beyond racism'" (Moiz par. 1). "It portrays the romanticization of blackness by white people as an object to be accumulated instead of a cultural identity to be understood. Although the film illustrates this negrophilia as a fantasization of blackness, it also reinforces the psychological struggle of black people trying to navigate through a larger racial dynamic where the white perspective either lionizes or demonizes black people, dictating the perception of black identity. The film also draws interesting parallels between what seem like the elements of a typical horror movie to real life events in order to reemphasize these ideas" (Moiz par. 1). Films are racial projects because of their racist portrayal of characters. Films, in most cases, can be used to train audiences to view race in various ways that may contribute to problematic color blindness, which shows how diverse the world we live in is and gives us an idea of the types of people whites portray us to be when they look at us. It insults and depresses Americans who still go through obstacles with racism everyday. This is one way that bigotry is taking place in the media.

Bigotry is also present in the media through music. Racist music is principally derived from the far-right skinhead movement and through the internet ("The Sounds of Hate" 2). The distribution of rock hate music via the internet has come to prominence since the establishment of a highly successful US online music distribution company ("The Sounds of Hate" 12). Racist music is also thought to be important in the recruitment of new members into racist groups. Examples of racist music include the album *Racially Motivated Violence* which contains songs entitled "Still Just a Nigger," "Race Mixing is Treason," "Mud Man," "Too White For You," and "Islam Religion of Whores" (Selepak 165-167). "Reports find that six in ten black music creators have experienced racism, while 86% say they have faced barriers to their career because of their race" (Savage par. 3). Bigotry put into music is up close and personal! A bigger problem is that people in the world today are highly uneducated on bigotry happening in the media today. According to Roger Wilson of the Black Lives in Music initiative, "Prejudice is here . . . There's nothing stealthy about it" (Savage par. 2). This is another way that bigotry is released into the media.

Lastly, bigotry is also present today through modern media and/or the internet. According to the University of Nevada, "We found that people of color are being targeted by organized misinformation efforts using digital technologies. We identified four primary racist discourses that operate on social media: stereotyping, scapegoating, allegations of reverse racism, and echo chambers" (Brown par. 5). Also, "Our research found that users utilize different ways to combat online racism. While both sites emphasized education and evidence, Twitter reactions featured more callouts, insults, and mockery than Reddit posts" (Brown par. 7). Structural racism in modern media is pernicious, and resolving it will require honest discussions, a more diverse workforce, and a confrontation of its roots in an ugly and discriminatory history. This is another way that bigotry in the media is taking place in the world.

In conclusion, bigotry in the media has become a major problem all around the globe and if people don't take action to educate themselves and others, it could possibly get worse as time goes by. Asking people questions about their beliefs allows for exploration of why they feel the way they do. These insights can help drive the conversation to resolve differences and open up loved ones and even strangers to new perspectives. If you or someone you know has experienced specific discriminatory acts, there are a number of resources available with information and mechanisms for reporting incidents.

Works Cited and Consulted

Brown, Melissa, et al. "Combating Racism on Social Media: 5 Key Insights on Bystander Intervention." *Brookings*, 1 Dec. 2021, www.brookings.edu/blog/how-we-rise/2021/12/01/combating-racism-on-social-media-5-key-insights-on-by-stander-intervention/, Accessed 27 March 2023.

Evelyn, Kenya. "How TV Crime Shows Erase Racism and Normalize Police Misconduct." *The Guardian*, 25 Jan. 2020, www.theguardian.com/media/2020/jan/25/law-and-disorder-how-shows-cloud-the-public-view-of-criminal-justice#::text=Distorting%20reality%3A%20crime%20shows%20misrepresent,-to%20how%20prosecutors%20are%20treated.

Fortino, Michael. "Fact or Fiction, Television Crime Shows Ignore Racism and Reality." *Criminal Legal News*, 18 Mar. 2020, www.criminallegalnews.org/news/2020/mar/18/fact-or-fiction-television-crime-shows-ignore-racism-and-reality/, Accessed 27 March 2023.

Moiz, Abdul. "*Get Out* Film Analysis — Negrophilia, Race-Relation and the New Dynamic." *Medium*. 25 Nov. 2019, medium.com/@abdulmoiz168/get-out-film-analysis-negrophilia-race-relation-and-the-new-dynamic-b64f6ed8095f, Accessed 27 March 2023.

Savage, Mark. "Racism in the Music Industry 'is Upfront and Personal." *BBC News*, 13 Oct. 2021, www.bbc.com/news/entertainment-arts-58884705, Accessed 27 March 2023.

Selepak, Andrew. "Power and Violence in Angry Aryans Song Lyrics: A Racist Skinhead Communication Strategy to Recruit and Shape a Collective Identity in the White Power Movement." *C&S São Bernardo do Campo*, v. 35, no. 1, p. 153-180, 2013, www.academia.edu/5195263/PowerandviolenceinAngryAryans-songlyricsAracistskinheadcommunicationstrategytorecruitandshapeacollec-tiveidentityintheWhitePowerMovement.

"The Sounds of Hate: The White Power Music Scene in the United States in 2012." *Anti-Defamation League*, 2012, www.adl.org/sites/default/files/documents/assets/pdf/combating-hate/Sounds-of-Hate-White-Power-Music-Scene-2012.pdf.

Usufzy, Pashtana. "Unpacking How Media Influences our Views on Racism." *We Need to Talk*, University of Nevada, Las Vegas. 26 Oct. 2020, www.unlv.edu/news/article/unpacking-how-media-influences-our-views-racism, Accessed 27 March 2023.

Racism in Memes on Social Media

Unless you do not go on social media at all, it's hard to miss how bad it has gotten over the last decade or so. Have you noticed how easy it is for someone to post something on social media? I mean just anything, but especially the memes that have gotten out of control, from the sexist to the most racist things that will shock us. Somehow you can get on a social media site and be bombarded with meme after racist meme. It seems like once one gets taken down one hundred get put back up in its place, so much so that I think people just get used to seeing the memes. Racism and bigotry should not be so normal that nobody says anything about it anymore. I refer to this type of meme as an "internet meme." Racism within memes has gone down over the years, but is not gone and can be seen while scrolling around.

Racist memes have gone down over the years, but they are not gone. According to Injeong Yoon,

> Overt Jim Crow racism is rarely found on social media and public platforms; there has been a decline in overt racist talk (Bonilla-Silva, 2006). This might explain why one of my students challenged me about showing racist Disney movie clips in art class. The student argued that the video they showed was out-dated, and we no longer see "that kind of racism" these days. I agreed with him in the sense that the video clips were from the 1970s and 1980s; from our current perspectives, the clips were extremely and obviously racist. However, I did not agree with his idea that we are no longer exposed to racism in the media. Overt racist discourse has been replaced with covert colorblindness (92).

There are racist memes out there. For example, see Figure 1 and Figure 2. Social media memes, in particular, are worse because people can post anonymously and regular folks can still hide their racism in public, expressing their hate and bigotry on social media platforms. One of the ways they do that is through memes. The memes in Figure 1 and Figure 2 are not as bad as the ones I have been seeing, particularly since 9/11. I've been noticing that memes have been getting more racist and if you look at the comments under the meme, the amount of people agreeing with the meme would shock many more than the meme itself, and that is sad. When you see that so many people agree with racist memes, it just gets worse and worse, and you see less being done about it. On social media, every race and religion is a target for becoming a meme. What is surprising is the amount of people who support it.

The internet and social media has changed so much since 9/11, and not in a good way. More people came out of all corners of the world knowing they could hide behind their computers. It seems like internet memes didn't miss anyone in particular when it came to racism and flat out hate. Everyone became equal opportunity, and some more than others depending on the current events in the country at the time. I have seen memes on social media websites that made me want to look away, and some that made my jaw drop in disbelief. People and groups can finally express how they really feel through social media discreetly, so they go all out and call it freedom of speech. I am not sure who regulates and rules over each media outlet, but there should be some strict or stricter rules and fines or even laws passed against bigoted, hateful, and outright mean content. On the other hand, there's that freedom of speech thing, so maybe that's why it's gotten worse or nothing has been done. Taking down or blocking people from social media for racist memes or content is not enough because, in minutes, a new profile can be made and the same content and memes will be shown over and over. A law should be passed in the future, and all the racism and hate that floods social media will all go away.

I heard this is funny but also scary 😩

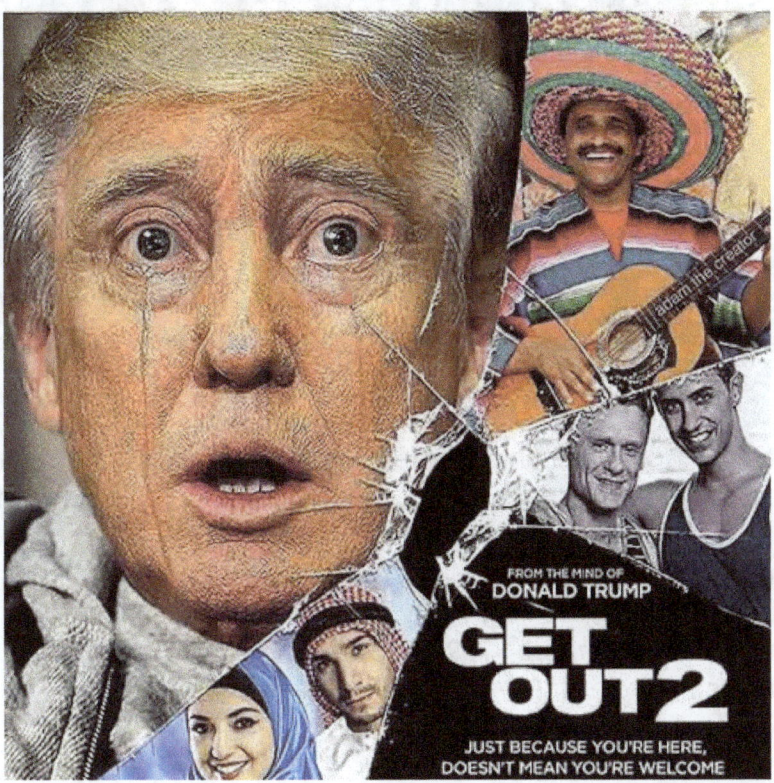

Figure 1

Figure 2

Works Cited

Daniels, Nicole. "Do Memes Make the Internet a Better Place?." *The New York Times*, 11 Feb. 2020, www.nytimes.com/2020/02/11/learning/do-memes-make-the-internet-a-better-place.html.

Turner, Mike. "50 Most Offensive Meme - Meme Central." *Meme Central - Best Funny Memes Collections*, 14 Oct. 2021, memecentral.org/offensive-memes/.

Yoon, Injeong. "Why is it not Just a Joke? Analysis of Internet Memes Associated with Racism and Hidden Ideology of Colorblindness." *Journal of Cultural Research in Art Education*, vol. 33, 2016, pp. 92–123, journals.librarypublishing.arizona.edu/jcrae/article/4898/galley/4839/view/.

Tina Hannah

Cyber-Racism

"It's clear that the media does a wonderful job at influencing the way society is seen and people who live in society [learn] how the media sets thoughts or images for you without you realizing it" (Wilder par. 1). Black people have always experienced racism in the media, but with new technological platforms, the reach of racism is very widespread. Because people of color cannot change the color of their skin, society has to do a better job of breaking down stereotypes and the perpetuation of racism in the media as a whole. You also see a lot of activists use mass media to try to keep their communities informed, and they do not see themselves as journalists, but they are performing acts of journalism. And more black journalists spoke up last year than any other time in recent history, leading major newsrooms to reckon with their histories of racism. Here, I will examine the problem of racism on the internet, or "cyber-racism," as well as illustrate the types of internet material that are of concern to racial equality and human rights groups in this country and international community.

"I find that when people discount factors like 'climate change is real' or 'systemic racism is real' it's for one of two reasons: One it's an issue of ignorance and lack of knowledge, but it can also be because they feel threatened" (Usufzy par. 27). Understanding how people respond to racial abuse online has broader implications for effectively constructing healthy communication, calming anger and frustration, and changing attitudes. They found the people of color are being targeted by organized misinformation efforts using digital technologies. We identified three primary racist discourses that operate on social media: stereotyping, allegation of reverse racism, and echo chambers.

For example, LSU women's basketball star Angel Reese won the national championship and the most outstanding player award at the Women's Final Four on Sunday, April 2, 2023, and made a gesture that has sparked much debate, especially on social media. Some have criticized Reese, while others defended her actions, highlighting how there was no public outrage in response to Caitlin Clark's gesture earlier in the tournament. Reese referenced the difference in reaction she received as a result of her gesture as compared to the one Clark received. Reese said, "All year, I was critiqued for who I was. I don't fit the narrative. I don't fit the box that they want me to be in. I was too hood. I was too ghetto. But when other people do it, they don't say anything" (Morse par. 6).

Now how is that? The media is for a fact throwing out racial behavior in our community, and it's not fair how people of color are still not being treated equal in this society. The topic of media influencing racism in our society is significant in research. It targets media bias, and therefore it is wise to explore how the media contributes to racism in explicit ways.

Some African Americans struggle to represent their own stories, beliefs, opinions, and identities because White people control the entertainment industry and choose what images of Black people to portray. Racism has become both ubiquitous and unrecognizable, precisely as its meaning is subjected to the never-ending and open-ended debates on social media and mass media. In fact, racism is increasingly debated through media events.

Works Cited

Morse, Ben. "Angel Reese Defends Gesture Directed Towards Caitlin Clark After LSU National Title Win; Calls out Double Standard After Being 'Unapologetically' Her." *CNN*, 3 April 2023, www.cnn.com/2023/04/03/sport/angel-reese-gesture-caitlin-clark-lsu-iowa-spt-intl/index.html.

Usufzy, Pashtana. "Unpacking How Media Influences Our Views on Racism." *We Need To Talk*, University of Nevada, Las Vegas, 26 Oct. 2020, www.unlv.edu/news/article/unpacking-how-media-influences-our-views-racism.

Wilder, SeMarial. "Racism in the Media: How the Media Shapes our View of People of Color in Society." *Community Engagement Student Work*. vol. 46, Merrimack ScholarWorks, 2020, scholarworks.merrimack.edu/soestudentce/46, Accessed 5 April 2023.

Angie Rosales Vazquez

Misrepresentation in the Media

The definition of race is often based on physical characteristics such as skin, hair texture, or eye shape. Culture is in the media, and the media has a huge influence on the way different races are viewed by society. Media misrepresentation consists of radio, film, magazines, and other media that gives a false representation with intent to deceive or to be unfair, that is still going on in today's world.

Most do not have interactions with many different people on a daily basis, but their discrimination is based on the image portrayed by the media. Kira Schacht wrote, "But, as Hollywood has featured more black characters and cast more black actors, it has also emphasized other stereotypes. To this day, black men are often portrayed as scary or angry and black women as loudmouthed and sassy. If a movie features one token black character, it's likely to be the black best friend. And, if people die in a movie, the black character is still likely to go first. Even with awareness of racial stereotypes rising, Hollywood persists with these tropes" (par. 16). Black characters usually die first. We live in a society in which the media has such a great influence on us, yet the influence is only in certain aspects and on certain people. Opinion news outlets, as well as other forms of media, benefit white people by glorifying them in every shape or form. People that do not go out of their houses and interact with the outside world are only informed of what happens through media, which is oftentimes biased.

Films and shows grind racial minorities into a specific social problem that is related to the color of their skin. According to Schacht, "Hollywood history provides many examples of racist caricatures. Black and Asian people have been repeated targets. Take the 1961 Audrey Hepburn movie *Breakfast at Tiffany's* and the bucktoothed Mr. Yunioshi, whose stereotypical "Engrish" accent was intended to mock Japanese people. He is notorious, and there are so many more examples" (par. 2). It can be said from the current popular culture that this stereotype still exists in our society. The film's and other outlets' harmful stereotypes are oftentimes created. One of the many challenges that American cinema endures is the inability to correctly portray characters of color and, unfortunately, this is still done in movies and shows in today's society.

The situation has not gotten any better, but rather it only either stays the same or gets worse. Not many people feel the need to talk about it or bring it up on TV, or in conversation, in my opinion, because it is something that is just looked over and swept under the rug. We can write about it, yes, we can talk about it, we can even fight about it, but I feel that it will not change anything. No, it is not a fair situation. No, it is not something we like to talk about or an easy conversation, but I seem to feel like media has not gotten any better about this stereotyping.

Works Cited

Schacht, Kira. "What Hollywood Movies do to Perpetuate Racial Stereotypes." *Deutsche Welle*, 21 Feb. 2019, www.dw.com/en/hollywood-movies-stereotypes-prejudice-data-analysis/a-47561660, Accessed 28 March 2023.

Haitham Mohammad

Racism Running Rampant

The concept of media reinforcing racism has become more rampant in historical stories, beliefs, and patterns. The level to which an individual exposes themselves to media consumption significantly impacts how they perceive society. According to "Time Flies," a report released by *Nielsen* in 2018, adult audiences spend over ten and a half hours daily on media consumption (par. 3). In the initial days of film and media, Black people faced challenges representing their beliefs, identities, stories, and opinions since White people had full authority in the entertainment industry and chose characters to portray Black citizens. Bigotry in the media can be seen through the facets that reinforce racism, including the production of Hollywood movies and biased news sources.

In modern days, similar trends are witnessed in media, influencing racial biases based on color, thus resulting in racial profiling, stereotyping, and microaggressions that impact society. Media facets continue reinforcing racism through coverage of crime reporting, police shootings, and racial profiling of Black, Asian, and Middle Eastern people. Therefore, a link exists between the historical media racial bias to the present depiction of racism in the media facets. Reporting crimes by television and broadcast media has continued being a debate since the historical inception of racial bias conflicts. Nowadays, news content to be aired on television has faced criticism for how Middle Eastern and African Americans are portrayed and targeted in reporting. In the article by Gutsche, hashtags have been increased that depict the symbolic annihilation of racism in calling 911 on Black people (par. 2). This use of hashtags has elevated the racial incident's coverage in ways that incriminate Black and Middle Eastern people to racial bias, since the crimes committed by African Americans, Asians, and other races are allotted much more in-depth and comprehensive visual content than those of White citizens.

Furthermore, according to a report by Euro-Med Monitor's team, racism and Orientalism have been widely reported by Middle Eastern journalists on the recent Ukraine crisis coverage, where the Western media coverage and stories tend to compare the Middle Eastern people from Europe and America based on color ("US and European Media" par. 1-2). For instance, most comments echoing on television depict Afghanistan citizens fleeing their countries as migrants or neighbors, but those fleeing from the Middle East as refugees or invaders. These comments are clear evidence of discriminatory policies that have existed throughout history ("US and European Media" par. 7). This problem calls for considerations about the perception of the public and racial groups' stereotypes, which the media directly impacts. Therefore, facets of media reinforce racism by stereotyping Middle Eastern people as invaders, further exacerbating society's perception of people of color.

Moreover, the media continues reinforcing racism in society through targeted bias. It is worth noting how facets of media reinforce racism in various ways. Nancy Yuen elaborates on ways media producers get negatively impacted by their race perceptions in creating content for the public, especially in producing Hollywood movies (par. 3). According to Yuen's argument, some producers currently work on providing content that accelerates racial inequality rather than a healthy bias. Most television and news stories nowadays tend to feature content depicting Black and Middle Eastern citizens in a wide range of social issues ranging from poor housing, violent crimes, and other expensive social welfare systems. It is worth noting that negative racial attitudes are directly linked to biased media. Therefore, it is wise to note that the negative racial bias portrayed by the media reinforces racism, which affects the way people interact with each other in society as influenced by the content in the media.

Lastly, mass media reinforces racism by promoting racial profiling. The lack of diverse and accurate representation of Black citizens in the media impacts how the public perceives and interacts with them. According to Balko, the conception of the Jim Crow era in the modern criminal system has helped reinforce racism in the United States. Most news stories recently have been covering police shootings of Black people who are not armed, thus becoming a primary theme cutting across multiple media platforms in terms of news. For instance, the murders of Trayvon Martin, Botham Jean, and George Floyd as the cause of racial profiling has been rampant in the US and hitting the headlines in the media (Balko). This racial order system has left African Americans presumed and judged guilty of offenses they did not commit, affecting how White people relate to them. To justify their identity, Black people tend to utilize channels that are non-threatening to White society, such as the inception of the Black Lives Matter movement. The derogatory remarks that commentators echo on television about Black and Middle Eastern people lead to increased inhumane acts and suffering, which becomes a norm in society. Therefore, having insight into how racism in the media creates a discriminatory society is important in identifying how media reinforces racial profiling and elevates systemic racism.

Bigotry in the media can be seen through the facets that reinforce racism, including the production of Hollywood movies and biased news sources. It is worth noting that media racial bias is a reflection of the long-withstanding marks from traumas of the past. Racial profiling, crime reporting, and targeted reporting are among the central themes in media platforms' news stories which have detrimental effects in accelerating the public perception and interaction with people of color. Based on research, Black people depicted as criminals, aggressive, and dangerous impact society's beliefs and ideology as they stereotype Black men. Therefore, the facets of media impact racism by enhancing stereotypes and racial bias in content and audience choice.

Works Cited and Consulted

Balko, Radley. "There's Overwhelming Evidence That the Criminal Justice System is Racist. Here's the Proof." *The Washington Post*, 10 June 2020, www.washingtonpost.com/graphics/2020/opinions/systemic-racism-police-evidence-criminal-justice-system/.

Freeman, Joshua. "Something Old, Something New: The Syndemic of Racism and Covid-19 and Its Implications For Medical Education." *Family Medicine*, vol. 52, no. 9, Society of Teachers of Family Medicine, Oct. 2020, doi: 10.22454/FamMed.2020.140670.

Gutsche, Robert E., Jr, et al. "#DiminishingDiscrimination: The Symbolic Annihilation of Race and Racism in News Hashtags of 'Calling 911 on Black People.'" *Sage Journals*, vol. 23, no. 1, 9 May 2020, doi.org/10.1177/1464884920919279.

"How US and European Media Language is Used to Describe the Ukrainian Crisis Reflects Deeply Rooted Racism Against Non-European Refugees." *ReliefWeb*, 13 May 2022, reliefweb.int/report/world/how-us-and-european-media-language-used-describe-ukrainian-crisis-reflect-deeply-rooted.

"Time Flies: U.S. Adults Now Spend Nearly Half a Day Interacting With Media." *Nielsen*, July 2018, www.nielsen.com/insights/2018/time-flies-us-adults-now-spend-nearly-half-a-day-interacting-with-media/, Accessed 21 July 2022.

Yuen, Nancy. "How Racial Stereotypes in Popular Media Affect People — and What Hollywood Can Do to Become More Inclusive." *Scholars Strategy Network*, 4 June 2019, scholars.org/contribution/how-racial-stereotypes-popular-media-affect-people-and-what-hollywood-can-do-become.

Kevin Vazquez

Racism in Society

Racism is still a very big topic in today's society, and people wonder when it will end. We've had plenty of cases where racism has been dealt with within these past couple of years. Some that even led to deaths. My three main thesis points will be about how racism is experienced in school, in workplaces, and in the community.

Racism is worldwide and the only way we know is through the media. When you're different from a certain pile, you get picked on. One student said, "I stopped loving myself because I realized the community did not love who I actually was" (Samuel and Wellemeyer par. 3). School is a place of education, yet it makes a person feel they have more than just education to go up against. For so long, history has fought for equal rights between schools and now you see schools mainly with their own people.

Being an adult and having to deal with racism in workplaces is the worst thing! People feel they have power over you, so they say anything. My skin color is what people base me off of, not how well I work. Janelle Coleman states, "It's hard because standing up for yourself in a moment like that makes you the angry Black woman" (Wagner par. 4). Anything can be used against you when you speak up, and the risk of losing your job is high.

Racism is in the community, I'm pretty sure we've witnessed it a couple of times in our lives. Now that it's a big thing and people are starting to make movements about it, people keep it to themselves. But that doesn't stop people from being racist. There have been plenty of cases opened when it comes to cops killing black lives. George Floyd was a case that shocked everybody. They cuffed him and put their knees on his neck, which stopped him from breathing.

Racism is a disease that people base on one person. They don't like this person, so they believe they are all alike. If you don't look like them, you're an easy target. The community is so against each other and battling one another that they don't realize the real issues of the world. Then again, the world is just a part of sin and this is all one big sin. Always be kind to one another; there is more after this life.

Works Cited and Consulted

The Associated Press. "Two Former Police Officers are Sentenced for Violating George Floyd's Civil Rights." *NPR*, 27 July 2022, www.npr.org/2022/07/27/1113991207/george-floyd-civil-rights-police-sentenced.

Samuel, Isoke, and James Wellemeyer. "Black Students Experience Trauma From Racist Incidents at School, Experts Say." *NBCNews*, 4 July 2020, www.nbcnews.com/news/nbcblk/black-students-experience-trauma-racist-incidents-school-experts-say-n1232829.

Wagner, Mike. "'Can't Let it Defeat You': Black Women's Stories of Racism Faced in Corporate America." *The Columbus Dispatch*, 3 Dec. 2020, www.dispatch.com/in-depth/news/2020/12/03/ohio-black-women-corporate-racism-sexism/3635647001/.

Monika Williams

Racism in Nursery Rhymes

Nursery songs were created to soothe, teach, and entertain children. Nursery rhymes were first invented in the 16th and 17th centuries. Racism can be found within today's old nursery rhyme songs. Many songs that we know today and loved from our childhood have racism embedded. These songs I used to sing as a kid, and enjoyed singing them. Racist nursery songs should be removed from children's learning experience, language skills, social skills, and conversational practice. There are five examples of songs that include slavery in their lyrics. To shed light, here are three racist nursery rhymes and alternatives that should be sung instead.

1. "Eenie, Meenie, Miny, Moe"

According to the article, "5 Nursery Songs That Are Actually Really Racist and Should Be Removed From Every Child's Learning Routine" by Tyler Marie, "A very popular nursery rhyme also used when playing tag as a sing-along for eliminating who will be 'it,' was originally a song about catching slaves" (par. 4). This can affect the community because if children really know the real words to this song they will be shocked and confused as to why this song was even made the way it was. This is talking about catching N*****s by their toes and letting them go. Which is harsh and I hope that all races teach their kids that racism is not a good look, it's mean and evil. It could get someone hurt or worse. All races don't like to be called other harmful names and that is understandable. If you want respect, you have to give respect, and I'm hoping parents are teaching their children this. I'm also hoping that parents who let their children listen to baby nursery songs are letting their children know the real meaning behind these songs so they won't be confused.

2. "10 Little Monkeys"

According to Tyler Marie, "This nursery rhyme, intended for counting fingers and toes, was originally a reference to Black people. All that changed was replacing the word n*****s or 'darkies' with the word monkeys. When you think of it, 'monkey' isn't really a better alternative, but 'One for the Money' is" (par. 5). This can affect the community just as it does right today. Why? Black African Americans do not like to be called "monkeys" or "N***r." We are not animals, we don't deserve to be called mean things. We have been labeled so much that it is a big problem in the world when it comes down to racism. I don't care what color a person is, we are all human and we all have to set a better example for children. Teach them to love all kinds of colors no matter what. Racism is wrong and I hate that it affects our community and that it is really parents that teach their children to be racist which is very dangerous and mean.

3. **"Do Your Ears Hang Low?"**

According to Tyler Marie, "The common tune often associated with the ice cream truck, was actually created and popularized by minstrel show performers mocking and profiting off of Black people. The original song entitled 'N****r Love a Watermelon Ha! Ha! Ha!' perpetuates the stereotype that Black people are obsessed with watermelon. A much more respectful alternative is 'The Elephant,' which shares lines and rhythm with 'Miss Mary Mack'" (par. 6). This can affect the community because I loved watermelon, especially as a kid. And because it says "N****r loves watermelon," it's making fun of black people. Not only do blacks love watermelon but all races love watermelon. Watermelon is about the best fruit to eat. It's really good and sweet. They just changed the words so that no one knows but all you have to do is research.

When I had kids, I didn't listen to nursery songs or didn't sing them to them. When my fourth child was born, she got hooked on the nursery rhymes and that is when I realized that the songs were kind of off to me. It didn't sound right to me, especially the "Baa, Baa, Black Sheep" song. Parents need to be mindful of the songs they play around children. I had to learn this for myself by having four children. Music can go a long way with words and actions. I've also taught my children to love all races; it doesn't matter what color someone is, everybody deserves to be loved and respected.

These nursery rhymes have racism embedded within the lyrics. Some nursery rhymes, like "The Itsy Bitsy Spider" and "I'm a Little Teapot" incorporate hand signs and movements to help children develop or enhance their motor skills, all while having fun. However, as helpful as nursery rhymes may be, some have origins that are not as pure, particularly in relation to black people. These nursery rhymes should be cut from schools. Let's change the narrative today.

Work Cited

Marie, Tyler. "5 Nursery Songs That Are Actually Really Racist And Should Be Removed From Every Child's Learning Routine." *Blavity*, 14 Sept. 2019, blavity. com/blavity-original/5-nursery-songs-that-are-actually-really-racist-and-should-be-removed-from-every-childs-learning-routine.

Clarissa Lugardo

Tolerating Child Abuse

Something we don't talk about enough or pay attention to nowadays is what kids are exposed to. We might think just because something is on parental controls that our kids are safe from indecent exposure. The truth is that there is a lot of sexualization our children are being exposed to through cartoons, TV shows, and movies that we would deem innocent. More and more studies are coming to light about this specific topic. Child abuse is becoming the new normal! This sexualization can cause low self-esteem, physical and mental health issues, and predatory behavior towards children, but parents can fight against this from occurring.

I'm sure you're wondering what, how, and why sexualization would be aimed at our children. Well, "Sexualization is the process whereby characters are portrayed and treated in an overly sexual manner" according to Elizabeth McDade-Montez (par. 3). As a young girl, I adored all of the Disney Princesses from Jasmine in the movie *Aladdin* to *Pocahontas*. I even have memories of clicking and clacking in my plastic glass slippers and playing in my pretend makeup, feeling like the prettiest princess. Walking in heels and wanting to wear makeup seemed so innocent. According to *The American Psychological Association*, sexualization occurs when any of these four aspects occur: a person's value derives solely from sexual behavior or sex appeal, excluding any other characteristics; a person is held to a narrowly defined standard that equates physical attractiveness with being sexy; a person is objectified sexually — valued only for others' sexual use — instead of seen as someone capable of acting independently and making decisions; and/or sexuality is imposed on a person inappropriately, as in the case of sexualizing children (Zurbriggen 1). I felt the pressure growing up, being manipulated into thinking I needed to wear makeup to feel pretty, trying to live up to those princess standards. That is why it's important to understand what sexualization is, how it's promoted to our youth, and how to prevent it. It comes in all colors, shapes, and forms, just like our children.

Sexualization can affect our children in so many ways. For example, it can harm their physical and mental health, creating self-esteem issues, eating disorders, and depression. Look at the child actresses such as Lindsay Lohan and twin actors Mary-Kate and Ashley Olsen. They have all dealt firsthand with alcoholism, drugs, and eating disorders most of their lives. Trying to live up to the expectations to stay thin, young, and beautiful. "A number of researchers have documented that what children are exposed to through media affects a variety of health behaviors including sexual activity, substance use, and aggression" (McDade-Montez, par. 8). In an article by Lois Collins, she states, "As an experiment, researchers gave some grade school-aged girls a sexualized doll, 'Fashion' Barbie, then asked the children about their career aspirations. Girls who played with the Barbie doll had fewer goals than the girls who instead played with Mr. Potato Head, who has no sex appeal . . . Her research found sexualized girls think they should pay attention to how their bodies look and they expect boys to focus on their bodies, too, and not on other attributes" (par. 12, 15). Instead of making education, goals, and self-value a priority, young girls feel the need to worry more about their appearances. It causes the children to grow up fast.

Sexualization of children can cause predatory behavior. All in all, it's not just princesses used to sexualize our children. It even dates back to public icons like Shirley Temple, making it easy for predators to justify their actions. There was a movie on Netflix that caused controversy last year called *Cuties*, that really showed us that sexualization is very serious. These young girls wear revealing outfits and dance in twerking routines with heavy makeup on. I couldn't even get through it without feeling enraged at how much they were exposed. Imagine other little girls looking up to that movie and the influence it could have on them. That is why we have to take action to prevent it.

Parents need to take action. According to McDade-Montez, "Parents, educators and children can take steps to counter messages of sexualization. Adults can teach children to value others for who they are, rather than for their looks. Adults can also encourage and provide activities that emphasize talents and abilities rather than appearance . . . Parents can pay attention to what their children watch and voice their concerns and opinions with their children's choices. For example, if your child wants to watch a show that you feel is sexualizing, share your thoughts and have a conversation about these ideas" (par. 11, 12). Other things you can do in my personal opinion is push more books onto our children. Limit screen time and monitor what they watch. Do things like board games, art projects, or maybe some fun at the park such as exercising or playing sports.

This sexualization can cause low self-esteem, physical and mental health issues, and predatory behavior towards children, but parents can fight against this from occurring. It's easy for us to just put the TV on and put our children in front of the screen. There's no wrong or right answer to parenting, but as a parent, we will always have the best interest at heart for our children. It's instinct to protect our young. Sexualization has become almost normal. Let's take the steps that we must to ensure our youth are healthy and happy. That is why we must stand up to sexualization and have zero tolerance.

Works Cited

Collins, Lois M. "How Sexualization of Girls Creates Long-Term Problems That Harm All Children." *Deseret News*, 17 Sep. 2020, www.deseret.com/indepth/2020/9/17/21432749/media-netflix-cuties-sexualizes-girls-tv-video-games-toys-sexual-harassment-assault/.

McDade-Montez, Elizabeth. "My Take: Sexualization in Children's Media." *ETR*, 3 Feb. 2015, www.etr.org/blog/my-take-childmedia/.

Zurbriggen, Eileen L., et al. "Report of the APA Task Force on the Sexualization of Girls." *American Psychological Association*, 2007, www.apa.org/pi/women/programs/girls/report-full.pdf.

Shemar Parkes

Police Respond to Video of Man Gripping
Special Needs Black Man by the Throat

When will racism stop in the United States of America? Will America ever be at peace? Is it possible for all black and white people to get along and come together for a better future? Will it ever happen? Because, over the years, black lives seem not to matter to either race, which is ridiculous to me because the world would be a better place and more peaceful if we all get along and don't pay attention to the color of skin. Racism is nasty and should not be this big of a problem worldwide. Social injustice and racism can be seen in the cases of Trevon Burks and Porter Burks.

On October 14, 2022, a young 24-year-old black man of the name Trevon Burks was accused of stealing a bike from a neighbor's yard when a 62-year-old Robert Walczykowski approached him aggressively and grabbed Trevon Burks' neck. He didn't have any proof whatsoever and then pleaded not guilty. Just a simple slap on the hand. This case was unjust and he should be held accountable for his action. Trevon Burks is a 24-year-old young man with special needs and that 62-year-old man knows better and knows what he is doing; he has no right to put his hand on nobody's kids.

Even in the video that took place, the witness was telling him to let his neck go. He's a kid (Womack par. 5). Nobody should be treated like that, but what can I say, African Americans be going through this for years and in some cases we get justice and in most cases we don't. We are all human and deserve to be treated with respect from all races. Black or white, we are all equal; no one is better than the other.

There was no justice in this case, just another case being handled with no justice.

"Detroit police fire 38 shots in three seconds, killing Black man . . . Porter Burks during a mental health crisis" (King).

"'In March of 2020, he stabbed two family members, a sister . . . he stabbed her in both her neck and her hand,' Graveline said at the news conference. 'As well as a brother in the top of his head as the brother came to defend the sister'" (King par. 13).

"'What we have found unfortunately is a system that has failed Mr. Burks on several different occasions,' Graveline said. 'That schizophrenia manifested itself into violent behavior. We have seen a pattern of him being brought to psychological services and being released and not being followed up with taking his medication'" (King par. 14).

"'The system failed Mr. Burks,' White said" (King par. 16).

I understand he had a knife, it still didn't give them the right to shoot at him 38 times in three seconds. Sometimes I feel like the law enforcement needs more requirements on their training. They have taser guns, why not use this instead of the gun? How fair is it that the officers could take his life? I don't think it was that serious to shoot him 38 times. Law enforcement or not, when will the world be at peace? What is the taser gun for? They need to be imprisoned for this crime; they're murderers and need to be punished for this. But reading into the article, it states that Burks stabbed his sister and other family. Why was the officer called to the scene? At this point I honestly don't know what to think.

Works Cited

King, Erica Y. "Detroit Police Fire 38 Shots in 3 Seconds, Killing Black man." *ABC News*, 5 Oct. 2022, abcnews.go.com/US/detroit-police-fire-38-shots-seconds-killing-black/story?id=91030791.

Womack, Kalyn. "Police Respond to Video of Man Gripping Special Needs Black Man By The Throat [Update]." *The Root*, Yahoo!News, 20 Oct. 2022, www.yahoo.com/news/video-milwaukee-man-grips-special-182018657.html?guccounter=1&gucereferrer=aHR0cHM6Ly93d3cuZ29vZ2xlLm-NvbS8&gucereferrersig=AQAAADBsr9EmyaQXMFLFmqWuKRIePdSh-h0u0qFpt9kfjpj3prvE3c5k6sOKe4JTtlfDTZ4w11az-hqZHj4cmmI23Dv-83vGF8eBb-MbeSEjokaF0fDblsAnzBuCqIDYsy9dkV3vOB54tJV8LI-Ca8R-jqDwUqwRI39Fa3B5PAMDNVMa.

Alaiah Outlaw Turner

Monsters in Uniforms

Godfrey David said, "I've been given this talk many times by many people. Don't be aggressive. Police usually work in groups of two: If you see one, assume there is one you cannot see. Nine times out of ten, people will believe the police over believing you. If a cop hits you, don't fight back: Hope that someone will notice and say something. Never match outfits: More than three men dressed in the same color equals a gang ..." (Igoe par. 5). The people that we grew up believing and praying will always save us and come to our rescue are the ones who are really killing us. Ousmane Zongo, Sean Bell, and George Floyd's lives were taken because of the color of their skin by police brutality. Justice was not served correctly for these men nor their families. Many black innocent lives are taken because racism still exists.

On May 22, 2003, Ousmane was inside of a warehouse when the police decided to perform a raid while investigating a CD scam. Ousmane was inside the warehouse at the time, working on his art, and had no idea what was about to take place. An undercover policeman dressed as a mailman was standing inside of the warehouse when he saw Ousmane turn on a light. The officer began to chase Ousmane, but at that time, the officer did not make it known that he was a police officer and still proceeded with the chase. The chase came to an end when Ousmane ran into a dead end. At this moment, he was shot four times in the back by the officer. After an investigation took place, the officer admitted that Ousmane had nothing to do with the raid and only ran because he was confused on why a mailman was chasing him. Ousmane was not in the wrong at all because any human would have ran if a person was chasing them for no reason. The officer was in the wrong in many different forms. For one, not identifying himself to Ousmane, and for two, wrongly killing him then later admitting that he knew Ousmane wasn't part of the raid, yet he still drew his weapon and killed him. A senseless, racist crime because he ran and was afraid for his life, and he was also a black man. The officer didn't get any jail time even after admitting he knew Ousmane should have not gotten killed; they gave him five years probation, and he lost his job, but that's all he received for taking a life. The whole judicial system fails many black people by either wrongfully incriminating them or not getting the correct justice that needs to be served. This is why racism still exists within the law.

Sean Bell was shot and killed the night before his wedding by a New York police officer. Sean and his friends went out one evening while Sean was hosting a party at a club that was under investigation. Officers in plain clothes followed Sean and his friends to their car, yet once again not identifying himself as an officer. The officer then yelled out to the other undercover officers that Sean and his friends were pulling away. At this time, the undercover officers shot into Sean's car over fifty times, killing Sean and wounding two of his friends. None of them had a gun, nor did they draw a gun on the undercover officers. People that know they have authority get too big-headed and use the badge or any other lawful jobs as an excuse to look down on other people, especially people of color. Black police killings have always taken place because an officer thought they saw a gun when in reality it's all racism, or maybe it's just as simple as "let's say we saw a gun," to get another black thug off the streets. Of course, they all work together, so it's their word over ours. Almost every person that has died because of a cop, in their report it says something about a gun, and even when they are wrong for killing, all they get is a slap on the wrist. This leaves the family heart broken and unable to trust in the police. Sean Bell didn't deserve to die the way he did, being unarmed and black was the cause. This is how racism still exists within the justice system.

On May 25, 2020, in Minneapolis, Minnesota, police were called to make an arrest because a store clerk told officers that George Floyd had made a purchase with a fake 20-dollar bill. Upon that arrest, officers were restraining Floyd in several unfit manners. Officer Derek Chauvin knelt on Floyd's neck for over nine minutes. Another officer pointed a gun at his head, all while Floyd was handcuffed and laying face down. Floyd wasn't fighting back and wasn't resisting arrest, but these are the measures that the police took in order to make sure he was down and that they had full control over him as the arrest was being made. Floyd started to complain about being claustrophobic and unable to breathe because the officer's knee was on his neck. After a while, Floyd had stopped talking, and he laid there motionless. The officers went to check him to find out he didn't have a pulse. All of this took place while the officer's knee was still on his neck. He died with the officer's knee on his neck. If Floyd's cry for help wasn't enough and him yelling, "I can't breathe" isn't enough to get the officer off of him, then I'm not sure what can be said to make these monsters believe our lives are in danger at their hands. This is how racism still exists within the justice system.

If there weren't any bystanders around to record what actually took place, then the officers would not have been charged with his death nor be able to wrongfully accuse him, making him guilty without even investigating what took place caused a man to lose his life. Automatically, they knew he was guilty and had to make a statement, not by the truth, but by the color of his skin, his height, by his demeanor, by his voice, by a lie. The officer's hands took a life that was innocent; a death that could have been prevented. There should have never been a gun pointed at his head or a knee on his neck. All of these actions that took place could have been prevented by a single conversation, but that didn't happen, because a life was taken by authority because they all believe they are better than us.

Black and white police officers abuse their authority. We have no choice but to be afraid of them only because we don't know how our life could end if in contact with these monsters. Growing up, we all know that monsters are bad, and we are terrified of them. We want our parents to come save us from these monsters. In all of the incidents that I talked about, unfortunately, their parents could not come save them. It couldn't happen. These aren't the only lives that were taken at the hand of the monsters, there are thousands of them, and some officers are yet still able to walk around and live their normal lives, see their families, and still have a job. "According to the FBI's data, 8% of the reported murders of Black people were committed by white offenders (234 of a total of 2,925) and 88.9% by Black offenders (2,600)" (Reuters par. 5).

As many people would say, "Don't look their way, don't talk to them." If you're ever in a situation when it's just you and them, please don't fight back because you might lose your life. Monsters come in many different shapes and forms and these are the ones that we should fear the most.

These monsters will never show their true colors, but we can! Not by fighting back, but by joining as one to help protect our lives and our children's lives and, hopefully, put a stop to the killings. We can march and we can pro-test, but we know we can never fight back with weapons or our hands be-cause then we are the monsters. Words are so powerful that they can change a generation; words can solve our problems. We know it's not going to happen overnight because it takes a village. Dr. King marched for equal rights years ago, and we still have to carry his legacy on because racism still exists to this day, and now, it's in the hands of those that were sworn in to protect us.

Works Cited

Igoe, Katherine J. "Black Lives Matter Quotes That are Powerful, Informative, and Necessary." *Marie Claire Magazine*, 29 April 2021, www.marieclaire.com/culture/a32823549/black-lives-matter-quotes/, Accessed April 23, 2023.

Reuters. "Fact Check: False Data on U.S. Racial Murder Rates." *Reuters*, 17 July 2020, www.reuters.com/article/uk-factcheck-data-racial-murder-idUSKCN24I2A9, Accessed 23 April 2023.

Mykayla Hall

Social Injustice

"I would like to be known as a person who is concerned about freedom and equality and justice and prosperity for all people," said Rosa Parks on her 77th birthday (Cramer par. 6). No black man should be brutally beaten by a police officer. Officers are supposed to protect and serve the community. Through police brutality and killing of black males, the Black Lives Matter movement came into the light. The murders of George Floyd, Rodney King, and Trayvon Martin were based on racism.

George Floyd

One recent event was the death of George Floyd. A 46-year-old man born in Fayetteville, North Carolina, on October 14, 1973. He died May 25, 2020, in Minneapolis, pinned to the ground in the hands of Officer Chauvin, making him the first white police officer in Minnesota to be charged with the death of a black civilian. It was so sad to see the video of George Floyd begging for his life saying he couldn't breathe and not one of the officers cared. They continued until he took his last breath with multiple bystanders around, setting off nationwide street protests of racial injustice and police brutality against African Americans. The demonstrations came in response to the killing of George Floyd (Olorunnipa par. 19). George Floyd's murder was a racialized police brutality killing, another black man dying at the hands of the law that's supposed to protect and serve against such racist acts.

Rodney King

"Twenty-five years ago this week, four Los Angeles policemen—three of them white—were acquitted of the savage beating of Rodney King, an African American man. Caught on camera by a bystander, graphic video of the attack was broadcast into homes across the nation and worldwide" (Krbechek par. 1). "Taken by bystander George Holliday from across the street, the footage shows four officers Tazing [sic], kicking, and hitting King with their batons upwards of 53 times" (Adams par. 4). I wonder what was going through the officers' heads as they brutally beat somebody's loved one—how cold-hearted. No black person should experience that pain of being severely beaten and being hospitalized with broken bones. This was seriously a racist act: four cops against one black man beating him severely, knowing that they would have not done that to a white person, or as I should say, to their own kind. So sadly, "Rodney King's death in June was the result of accidental drowning, although alcohol, cocaine, marijuana and PCP found in his system were contributing factors, authorities said" (Wilson par. 1). He was 47.

Trayvon Martin

"Fatal shooting of Trayvon Martin by George Zimmerman in Sanford, Florida, on February 26, 2012. The shooting exposed deep divisions among Americans on race issues" (Munro par. 1). Trayvon lost his life at a young age—he was only seventeen. The Trayvon Martin killing was also an act of racism. He was being profiled by a member of a neighborhood watch who tried to take matters in his own hands, following him as Trayvon Martin was coming from the store and wrongly accusing him of being a burglar in the neighborhood. Trayvon was innocent; he did not deserve to lose his life at the hands of a racist, heartless man who still continued to lie after the young man's death saying he was attacked; Trayvon Martin was unarmed.

The murders of George Floyd, Rodney King, and Trayvon Martin were based in racism. No black man should be brutally beaten by a police officer. Officers are supposed to protect and serve the community. Police, please do better. What if that was your loved one getting brutally beaten by an officer that's supposed to protect and serve? Live by your heart not by the badge, know your rights!

Works Cited

Adams, Cydney. "March 3, 1991: Rodney King Beating Caught on Video." *CBS News*, 3 Mar. 2016, www.cbsnews.com/news/march-3rd-1991-rodney-king-lapd-beating-caught-on-video/.

Cramer, Sarah. "#InContext: Rosa Parks." *Human Trafficking Institute*, 2 Aug. 2017, traffickinginstitute.org/incontext-rosa-parks/.

Krbechek, Anjuli Sastry, and Karen Grigsby Bates. "When La Erupted in Anger: A Look Back at the Rodney King Riots." *NPR*, 26 Apr. 2017, www.npr.org/2017/04/26/524744989/when-la-erupted-in-anger-a-look-back-at-the-rodney-king-riots.

Munro, André. "Shooting of Trayvon Martin." *Encyclopedia Britannica*, 31 Jul. 2024, www.britannica.com/event/shooting-of-Trayvon-Martin.

Olorunnipa, Toluse. "George Floyd." *Encyclopedia Britannica*, 7 Sep. 2024, www.britannica.com/biography/George-Floyd.

Wilson, Stan, and Alan Duke. "Police: Rodney King's 'Accidental Drowning' Involved Drugs." *CNN*, 23 Aug. 2012, www.cnn.com/2012/08/23/us/rodney-king-autopsy/index.html#::text=%E2%80%9CThe%20effects%20of%20the%20drugs,%2C%E2%80%9D%20the%20autopsy%20summary%20said.

Celebration: Reflections on Identity

Ryan Bonilla

Change My Ways

To the old me
I'm changing my ways
To the new me
Dig yourself out of the mental cave
Say goodbye to depression.
Old me, say hello to righteousness beyond the self
To my old friends that pulled me down
So long and sorry, but I'm changing my ways
Old me, with so much hate, I'm changing my ways
I am proud of this new me, I think we will get along pretty well.
GOD so thank you for helping me find a way to change my ways

CHANGE MY WAYS

"Change My Ways" is a poem about moving forward in a positive direction. It is about self-reflection and coming to terms with all the things internally and externally that got in the way of being a better person. The poem's theme is about leaving behind a negative past and becoming comfortable with the changes that lie ahead. This theme is present throughout the poem: "To the old me / I'm changing my ways" and "Old me, say hello to the righteousness beyond the self." The poem drives this theme halfway through with the line, "So long and sorry, but I'm changing my ways."

The poem promotes change in a very direct way. It is like a goodbye letter to the person who needed positive change, and to confront all of the negative things that caused problems. At the same time, the poem is welcoming change for this new, better person. For example, "Old me with so much hate, I'm changing my ways / I am proud of this new me, I think we will get along pretty well." This illustrates a changed outlook from negative to positive and even excitement for the positive change.

A free bird leaps
on the back of the wind
and floats downstream
till the current ends
and dips his wing
in the orange sun rays
and dares to claim the sky.

This passage, from Maya Angelou's "Caged Bird," goes with my poem because it's talking about how the bird is free with the wind on its back. The bird and my poem talk about the struggles of not being able to free yourself from people. "A free bird leaps / and floats downstream / and dares to claim the sky" (Angelou lines 1, 3, 7), means that with all your struggles, you can still reach for the sky. My poem also has the same meanings, from not being able to accomplish anything to being free.

Works Cited

Angelou, Maya. "Caged Bird." *Shaker, Why Don't You Sing?*, Random House, New York, New York, 1983.

Nicholas Henderson

Caged Bird

The piece I made shows a free bird and a jailed bird. It shows one bird locked in the cage and the other one flying free. The free bird is flying into the sunset with a worm in his mouth while the other bird is stuck in a cage crying and chained down. The caged bird wants to be free like the other bird but the bars are holding him back.

By looking at my art piece, you will see what Maya Angelou was saying when she said, "A free bird / floats downstream / till the currents / and dips his wings / in the orange sun rays" (lines 1, 3-6) and, "The caged bird sings / with a fearful trill / of things unknown / but longed for still / and his tune is heard / on the distant hill / for the caged bird / sings of freedom" (lines 15-22) in the form of a picture. The picture shows a free-minded person and a locked down-minded person. You will also notice the emotions from both birds. One is crying while the other is smiling and flying to the sunset. The caged bird just wants to enjoy his right to be free like the other bird. But society clipped his wings and caged his mind.

My piece shows how blacks and whites were not treated equally. The caged bird represents the blacks and the free bird represents the whites. The black community was more caged because they were not able to move around and enjoy life without being judged and looked down upon. They had limited rights and were always handed the low end of the stick.

Works Cited

Angelou, Maya. "Caged Bird." *Shaker, Why Don't You Sing?*, Random House, New York, New York, 1983.

Stephanie Vazquez

If I Had Wings

If i had wings, I'd fly into the beautiful blue sky,
And drift into the jet stream, where the wind is wild and high,

I'd fly across the ocean with the birds by my side,
Using my beautiful furry wings to travel the sky,
Oh how lovely, i just want to fly,
With great velocity i fly and fly,

My heart would be so grateful and satisfy,
Flying all around the world, it will grow to fill the emptiness inside,
Filled with contentment from recognizing Grace and the beauty of life,

When all the world was traveled and nothing left to see,
I'd fly back home and rest my soul to sleep,

A now more humble and better me,
I fly and fly still in my dream.

This poem of change I created is to show that life can be beautiful no matter how you feel inside. Sometimes the emptiness we feel inside is not really so empty, we just have to learn how to fulfill ourselves with the grace of God. We have to be the ones to create our life. Be committed to what we want and work hard to achieve it. Fly high in the sky.

We may feel we aren't achieving much, but if we just cherish what we have and see that we have been creating a beautiful life since we were born, full of love and joy, we wouldn't think the same way. We need to change the way we think. We've created our own family whether it's your spouse, kids, dogs, etc.—we have a family, loved ones, and people who love us back. We have health and we are wealthy, but most importantly we have a life. We have to be thankful we've made it this far and we will continue to create the most wonderful times of our life journey that's left for us. A now more humble and better me.

The change in my poem is about changing the way we view things in life. "If i had wings, I'd fly into the beautiful blue sky." We have to change the way we see things, stop thinking that what we want is going to just come to us. Instead, we should go out and create the life we want. "Using my beautiful furry wings to travel the sky." See, we sit down and complain about what we don't have or what we could have had, but do we go out and get it!? Sometimes we hesitate about doing the things we want or maybe getting a better and healthy lifestyle, or even getting that purse that we hesitated on buying a couple weeks ago. We have to stop being hard on ourselves and live life to the fullest. I, as a mother, hesitate a lot on getting myself something I'd want or need. I'd rather spend that money on my son, like some socks, although I know I just bought him a couple pairs of socks a week ago. Or I beat myself up because I want to lose my stubborn fat, but don't motivate myself enough to go out and work out. I think we just have to stop putting excuses as to why we couldn't and start saying why I chose to do it. "When all the world was traveled and nothing left to see / I'd fly back home and rest my soul to sleep." And that's what I mean, we have to change the way we think and just go out and proceed with whatever is on your mind to do so.

My poem was inspired by a Maya Angelou poem called, "Caged Bird." This poem inspired me because this caged bird had a desire to be free, as my poem says, "Flying all around the world, it will grow to fill the emptiness inside" and his strength to dare claim the sky, "I'd fly across the ocean with the birds by my side." I feel like that's what we all need to do: claim the life we want and go out and get it without anyone stopping you. Have the strength to live the life you want without worrying what anyone says. It's okay to feel like the caged bird, but you also have to be the free bird that flies without fear.

"The caged bird sings / with a fearful trill / of things unknown / but longed for still / and his tune is heard / on the distant hill / for the caged bird / sings of freedom" (Angelou lines 15-22).

Works Cited

Angelou, Maya. "Caged Bird." *Shaker, Why Don't You Sing?*, Random House, New York, New York, 1983.

Dombanee Lincoln

Look Into My World

My visual arts project contains a form of expression that is my feelings, emotions, and imagination. I'm using my skills on how to draw while being creative. Everyday life people can choose to look at art in a negative or positive way. Art can be an inspiration to anyone who looks hard enough because art that has a message behind it is always more powerful and more important than art that's done only to look beautiful. Colors used in art may cause a reaction in people. Yellow is often called the brightest and most energizing of the warm colors. Green can represent new beginnings and growth. It's considered an earth color. Blue is used to represent calmness and responsibility, and is refreshing and friendly. Black is the strongest of colors on the positive side of power, elegance, and formality. On the negative side, it's used with evil, death, and mystery. Pink is playfulness, fun, and youthful; it makes you feel funky and futuristic. I'm translating my picture into words.

The goal is to help you understand the meaning of the picture and what it means to me. A person's eyes are the window to their soul. Your eyes can reveal the truth about you, even if you're lying with a straight face, your eyes can give you away. Art can be considered as a human activity—art connecting the artist to the world of colors. Artists use the art to express their feelings by showing their ideas and representing them on a platform. Through the arts, thoughts, feelings, and needs are communicated. It must be known that the cornerstone of this mode of therapy is psychoanalysis, which will be explored in detail below.

Art therapy has been supplementing the psychotherapeutic programs in the hospital settings. It is now widely used in psychiatric hospitals and rehabilitation centers, and is practiced by qualified art therapists or by psychologists. But when and how did it begin? To begin to understand the discipline of psychology and the role psychoanalysis played in the practice of psychotherapy in general, it is noteworthy to mention that while psychoanalysis and psychology have a common background in nineteenth century science, they were independent of one another for a number of years because of their differences in focus or interests. Psychology was looking at all elements and processes of sensation, perception, memory, and thinking.

Don't Judge a Book by Its Cover

Why do we as people judge others by the way they choose to dress? Realistically, does clothing tell you everything you need to know about a person? People seem to think a piece of material is a part of our flesh. As though the way we dress tells a story about a person. Many believe clothes define us and create who we are, but you should not judge a book by its cover.

People have different perspectives on the topic: does clothing define us? Clothing we choose to wear does not define who we are as individuals. I wear more scrubs than anything. What does that say about me? Am I a workaholic? According to *NursingUniforms.net*, "Nursing scrubs define your personality and tell people who you are. A well-fitted and styled set of matching nursing scrubs can make you stand out and make others take note of you. You will be seen as a confident nurse who cares about projecting the right image, when you are seen wearing a good set of scrubs" ("What Your Nursing Scrubs Say" par. 1). "If you prefer to wear only solid, dark color nursing scrub sets to work, people sooner or later associate you with a rather stable but boring personality. You will be seen as reliable and consistent but rather lacking in imagination. While this will not affect your career options, you might find yourself alone more often than not. Injecting a bit of color and a bit of unpredictability into your nursing scrub wardrobe now and then might loosen up your image with your coworkers" ("What Your Nursing Scrubs Say" par. 4). This is ridiculous. I would have never thought people think like this. Who goes to the uniform store and says, "Excuse me, I'm looking for the bubbly, I don't take life seriously but I'm a rich nurse look"? Sounds crazy right?

Some people believe clothes create who we are. According to *Forbes*,

What you wear can inform passersby of your type of employment, as well as your ambitions, emotions, and spending habits. And now it's even launched a whole new type of psychology.

Clinical psychologist Dr. Jennifer Baumgartner literally wrote the book on this phenomenon, which she calls the "psychology of dress." In "You Are What You Wear: What Your Clothes Reveal About You," she explains not only how psychology determines our clothing choices, but how to overcome key psychological issues your wardrobe might be bringing to light in your everyday life, or even at work (LearnVest par. 1-3).

I disagree because all humans express themselves in different ways and forms of clothing. We all have different perspectives. We can agree to disagree. Clothing does not define us as individuals, it can only be a costume to the character of the day.

I have been around enough people to know you can not judge a person by how they choose to dress. A person that is fashionable and is up to date with the latest trends can be struggling behind all the glam. A wealthy person can be seen wearing modern-day wear, comfortable with not being so flashy, and have a bank account that is well-maintained.

According to Bob Anderson,

> I've been around far too long to base wealth opinions solely on appearances. A mate of mine, Dan O'Neill, once lined up a meeting with someone he thought could be a good JV partner or investor. Dan asked me to meet him on the road adjacent to the 9th hole of a par 3 golf course. I assumed we would go from there to the person's office. I got there early and waited for Dan. The 9th hole and a few bunkers were just over the fence, so I struck up a conversation with the old groundskeeper. He was a suntanned, wiry old bugger with as many teeth as gaps. He had been raking the bunker before throwing his rake in the back of a rusty old Datsun 1600 UTE. After a good convo about the weather and fishing Dan arrived, early for the first time in his life. 'I see you've already met Ted,' he said – and they both smiled. It turned out Ted owned the golf club, had just sold the adjoining land for $40M, owned 900 acres of future development land two kilometers away, had $50M invested with Comsec etc. It turned out he was worth $200M with no debt (par. 9-12).

This is a prime example of the phrase, "don't judge a book by its cover." You might miss out on an amazing person. Let's normalize not being so judgmental of others.

Many believe clothes define us and create who we are, but you should not judge a book by its cover. Does spending a significant amount of money on an outfit make you rich? Does dressing basic make you poor? Judging people on the clothing they choose to wear would be closed-minded and naïve. A person making six-figures could be rich with basic fashion and someone working minimum wage could have six-figure fashion. You cannot know a person's life story by clothing. Some people are materialistic while others are comfortable living the simple life. Looks can be deceiving. Don't judge a book by its cover.

You might miss out on an amazing person. Let's normalize not being so judgmental of others.

Works Cited

Andersen, Bob. "Appearances Can Be Deceiving." *LinkedIn*, 2 March 2021, www.linkedin.com/pulse/appearances-can-deceiving-bob-andersen.

LearnVest. "What Your Clothes Say About You." *Forbes*, 14 April 2022, www.forbes.com/sites/learnvest/2012/04/03/what-your-clothes-say-about-you/?sh=2f9904596699.

"What Your Nursing Scrubs Say About You." A Nurse's World Blog, *Nursing-Uniforms.net*, www.nursinguniforms.net/blog/what-your-nursing-scrubs-say-about-you.

Yoana Vazquez

Clothing and Body Image

Clothing affects us in various ways. People like different styles of clothing depending on how clothes fit them. Everyone has a unique clothing style; not everyone is the same. Studies have shown clothing can affect our personality and mood, given the way the clothes fit you. Men have less attraction to clothing than women, and women dissatisfied with their bodies can lead to negative impacts on their self-image.

Clothing affects personality. "Why do people in the same social cultural environment choose certain clothing styles and not others?" (Stolovy par. 5). People choose certain clothing to wear. Clothes reflect personality and how people feel about themselves through what the person's style is and how the clothes fit them. Some people like to wear their clothing tight and others like them loose. Clothing can reflect the standard cultural values of a nation.

"Men have been shown to express less interest in clothing and fashion than women" (Stolovy par. 6). Men show less attraction towards fashion and clothing. All those women tend to have more desire for fashion and clothing; they actually select it more as camouflage if they feel too big or too small, and less for an individual's self-expression. Women are more into fashion, they love clothes and they love shopping. Men do not care so much about fashion, not like women do.

Women are dissatisfied with body image: "In other words, how individuals feel about and perceive their bodies" (Stolovy par. 8). Women who didn't like their bodies were more likely to disguise their bodies by wearing dark colors and baggy shirts, and they will avoid showing a lot of skin or wearing tight-fitting clothing. The better the women or men feel about their bodies, the higher their ability to wear clothing for assertiveness and self-enjoyment. Personal body image blends the thoughts and feelings that you have about yourself. Body image disagreements relate to body image dissatisfaction and negatively impacts mental health, including lowering self-esteem.

At the end of the day, I believe people should wear what they desire because nobody knows what the next person is going through. People shouldn't be judged by their clothing or appearance. Clothes reflect who you are, your personality, mood, and the style that you wear.

Works Cited

Stolovy, Tali. "Styling the Self: Clothing Practices, Personality Traits, and Body Image among Israeli Women." *Frontiers in Psychology*, vol.12, Frontiers, 8 Sep. 2021, doi.org/10.3389/fpsyg.2021.719318.

Mariah Bennett

Clothing Changes Our Perspectives

How do we represent the contradictions of society and ourselves in our everyday lives? "Through appearance and style (personal interpretations of, and resistances to fashion), individuals announce who they are and who they hope to become" (Kaiser par 1).

Clothing directly affects our mood, attitude, and confidence. It can enhance our psychological state and improve our performance tasks. We can achieve more when we feel we are dressed for the occasion. The style, material, color, and shape of our clothing choices can express different emotions. By wearing clothes we love, we feel confident in ourselves and this is particularly important for the well-being of others.

Clothing reflects on who you are and how you are feeling at the moment. It embodies personal wealth and taste. Clothing can provide protection from ultraviolet radiation. Clothing that doesn't fit well or fails to flatter someone can lead to poor body image. Wearing clothing designed to complement your unique figure can help to improve body image and confidence. Clothes reflect who you are, how you feel at the moment, and sometimes even what you want to achieve in life. Always remember that whatever you wear should reflect the real you. Your fashion sense reflects your personality, character, mood, style, and who you are as an individual. Clothes developed from a practical asset to a social marker. They affect the way we see ourselves. Clothes help us to be seen in the light that we wish to be seen and also execute our personalities and social status.

The color, comfort, fit, and style of our clothes can directly affect our confidence levels. Physical appearance plays an important role in an individual's life. If we appear vibrant and active, people in our surroundings will perceive us as a positive individual. If we wear untidy clothes, people will form an opinion that we give off negative energies.

Clothes being part of today's fashion and trends can tell us a great deal about a person's background, social status, aesthetic tastes, mood, and even about climatic conditions. They also show whether one is bereaved or not. You can most likely know about a woman's marital status by way of dressing. "Fashion becomes inextricably implicated in constructions and reconstructions of identity" (Kaiser par 1).

Works Cited

Kaiser, Susan B. "Fashion and Identity." *Love to Know*, www.lovetoknow.com/life/style/fashion-identity.

Jenevi Lal Par

Positive Influences Through Self-Expressive Fashion

Have you ever noticed how your mood and confidence levels can change when you put on a favorite outfit? Clothing is much more than a simple covering for our bodies; it holds the power to shape our identity and influence the way we are perceived by others. From the colors we choose to the styles we embrace, our clothing reflects our individuality and communicates messages about our personality and values. Our clothing choices are involved in defining our identity, influencing our behavior, and shaping the perceptions of others.

Self-Expression and Identity: Our clothing choices help as a powerful form of self-expression, allowing us to showcase our unique identities. According to "Self-Expression Through Fashion," "A person's wardrobe is an intricate reflection of their inner identity. It speaks volumes about who we are as individuals, with fashion being a vehicle for self-expression and connection to the external world. The way you dress can make all the difference in how you feel, from inspiring confidence, to boosting moods, making it undeniably important when navigating life" (par. 2). The clothes we wear can also reveal who we are as individuals including our interests, cultural background, and personal style. For instance, someone wearing a punk rock band t-shirt conveys a love for alternative music, while someone dressed in traditional attire celebrates their cultural heritage. By carefully selecting our clothes, we assert our individuality and communicate to the world who we are. This is how clothing can show self-expression and identity.

Influence on Behavior: Our clothing choices have the ability to influence our behavior and mindset. According to "7 Ways Your Clothes Change The Way You Think," "what we wear influences our behavior, attitudes, temperament, mood, assurance, and even how we communicate with others" (par. 3). This experience, known as "Enclothed Cognition," reveals that what we wear can impact how we view ourselves and how we behave. Our clothing choices can directly influence our behavior. Similarly, wearing athletic clothes can motivate us to engage in physical activities. By choosing our outfits, we can take the power of clothing to shape our emotions and actions. This is the reason why our clothing choice can directly influence our behavior.

Perception by Others: Our clothing choices also play a significant role in how others perceive us. "Clothing can also affect how others perceive us. When we wear clothing that is associated with a certain group or social class, others may treat us differently. For example, if someone wears a suit to a job interview, the interviewer may perceive them as more competent and professional," ("How Clothing Affects Behavior" par. 1). People often make judgments and beliefs based on how we look, including the clothes we wear. Dressing appropriately for a job interview, for instance, can create a positive first impression and increase the chances of success. Our clothing choices create a visual story that influences how others relate to us, forming the basis of initial perceptions. This is why our clothing choices shape the perceptions of others.

Our clothing choices are involved in defining our identity, influencing our behavior, and shaping others' perceptions. By selecting our outfits, we can express our individuality, impact our behavior, and manage the impressions we make on others. Let us accept the trend in clothing psychology and recognize the power of our clothing in defining who we are. So next time you choose an outfit, remember that your clothes are not merely fabric, they are a reflection of your true self. Dress with intention and let your clothes tell your story.

Works Cited

"Self-Expression Through Fashion - IIFT Blog." *IIFT Bangalore*, 21 Feb. 2023, www.iiftbangalore.com/blog/the-art-of-self-expression-how-fashion-can-speak-volumes-about-you/. Accessed 21 October 2023.

Synerg. "How Clothing Affects Behavior and Social Perception?" *Synerg - The Clothing Manufacturers*, 28 April 2023, thesynerg.com/clothing/. Accessed 22 October 2023.

"7 Ways Your Clothes Change The Way You Think." *Calm Sage*, 26 Dec. 2022, www.calmsage.com/how-clothes-change-the-way-you-think/. Accessed 21 October 2023.

Xiomary Lee Rivera

Fashion Psychology

How do you feel when you wear your favorite outfit? Clothing psychology researches how clothing affects individuals. Also, how a person's daily mood affects how they dress and vice versa. Culture plays a big role in how people dress and what is expected. Through enclothed cognition, mind frame, and color uppers and downers, clothing affects us mentally.

Enclothed cognition assists in creating our reality. "Science says that the clothes we wear affect our behavior, attitudes, personality, mood, confidence, and even the way we interact with others. This is 'Enclothed Cognition'" ("Behavior and Clothing Choices" par. 2). Basically, based on what we are wearing, we attract different people. Different outfits bring out different sides of a person's personality. This is one way clothing affects us mentally.

Clothing sets our mind frame, depending on style type. "Their choice of clothing can help women overcome objectification and cultural body-ideal pressures, promoting self-validation and mastery" (Stolovy par. 1). Wearing what you want and feel is such a form of expression, and it's how you communicate without verbally speaking. An outfit and how a person wears it explains how a person feels about one's self in that moment, day, or in general. Confidence, energy, and attitude can all reflect on the things someone puts on; self-care starts with one's wardrobe! This is just the beginning on how your clothes can affect your mental state in any way, good or bad.

Colors within clothes can have an upper or downer effect on our mental state. "We even evaluate people whom we just met based on their clothes and the occasion," Sarda-Joshi said (par. 4). Based on my own experience, I understand the colors a person wears are either based on comfort zones or who they want to project themselves as in that moment. If a person is working, they are more than likely to have on solid or uniform type of colors and their mood might be a little off. When people wear nice bright colors, it's more uplifting, positive, and exciting energy to be around. Dressing in colors you see yourself wearing more of can be manifesting a new you, becoming a different person because you're confident in your clothes, body, and spirit. That's why I know clothing affects you mentally.

Through enclothed cognition, mind frame, and color uppers and downers, clothing affects us mentally. Enclothed cognition assists in creating our reality. Clothing sets our mind frame, depending on style type. Colors within clothes can have an upper or downer effect on our mental state. Next time you put on an outfit, consider it being a part of what affects your mood. Change accordingly to be more positive.

Works Cited

"Behaviour and Clothing Choices, Practices and Effect and Clothing on the

Individual." *Government Women College Gandhinagar*, gcwgandhinagar.com/econtent/document/15875365973.%20Behaviour%20and%20Clothing%20choices.pdf.

Sarda-Joshi, Gauri. "Psychology of Clothes: What You Wear Changes the Way You Think." *Brain Fodder*, brainfodder.org/psychology-clothes-enclothed-cognition, Accessed 26 July 2023.

Stolovy, Tali. "Styling the Self: Clothing Practices, Personality Traits, and Body Image among Israeli Women." *Frontiers in Psychology*, vol.12, Frontiers, 8 Sep. 2021, doi.org/10.3389/fpsyg.2021.719318.

Dechante Nelson

I Love You But . . .

Your parents are supposed to love you no matter what. That's what they say anyway. I used to wonder when I was younger how life would have been if I had lived with my dad, but that thought had gone away once I spent more time with him. I always knew the type of person he was. I just kept giving him chance after chance, because that's what we do with the people we want in our lives. That would soon come to an end, though, once he crossed a line I could never forgive him for.

Growing up, I didn't have my dad around until I was four years old and even then it was barely time spent. I remember nagging my mom about where my dad was because all the girls in school kept boasting about how their dad is taking them to the daddy-and-daughter dance. He lived in Minnesota at the time and one day he drove down here to Milwaukee to pick me up and take me back with him. I was so excited. I told all the kids in my school I wasn't going to see them ever again because I was moving to a new state. Everything was fine for the first few months. I met my little brothers, who are just a few years younger than I am. My step-mom at the time, who is my brothers' mom, had these big bins of Barbies and accessories just for me. My dad's mom, who goes by Peaches (I don't refer to her as my grandma), was also living there. I felt like I was complete because I finally met my other family. Little did I know the good wasn't going to last long.

When I was younger, my asthma was so bad that any movement or playing around I did, I'd have an asthma attack. I was laying in bed and all of a sudden my chest got tight and it felt as if I couldn't move at all. Dragging myself to his bedroom door and knocking as hard as I could for someone who was losing air, he never opened it for me until Peaches yelled his name. He threw my inhaler at me and told me to go back and lay down. I still have yet to get over that. I had him call my mom for me to go back home because I didn't feel safe anymore. It'd be years before I saw him again.

In third grade, I started to notice things about me that made me feel out of place with my peers. I started developing crushes on my friends who just so happened to be girls. I would purposely touch their hair, give them hugs, and always tried to play with the prettiest girl in school. I never told anyone except my best friend at the time. We were at her house having a sleepover. As we were watching *The Little Vampire*, I kissed her. She was quiet for a couple hours before she asked me why I did that. I told her I thought I liked girls. We kept the situation to ourselves because she didn't want to be called weird for letting a girl kiss her and I didn't want to be called weird for kissing her. We stayed friends until we parted ways for middle school.

As years went by and I started high school, I became a little more confident outside of home with who I was. I went to Milwaukee High School of the Arts and there I felt like I could be me because of how fluid the school was. Everyone was confident about who they were. They didn't need to hide. My mom started to notice some things about me and so did my aunt. I came out to my aunt first. My mom found out on her own and she was not happy. I had my first girlfriend my freshman year of high school at age 14. We texted each other all the time, found ways to hang out after school, and I even met her parents. My mom was going through my phone while I was doing my homework one night and found all of our messages. She was so distraught that she confiscated my phone and proceeded to call my dad, whom I had not seen since I was four years old, to come and pick me up for the summer. I was devastated. I had to break up with my first girlfriend who I was so proud to have.

Being in Minnesota was nothing short of being in Milwaukee. Although I did miss it, I just made myself comfortable there while I waited for the summer to be over. My dad was the regional manager for Wendy's at the time, so he was always gone and I'd be out adventuring and networking on my own. I met so many people in the LGBT community while I was there. It was refreshing being around my own. I was waiting for what felt like ages for my dad to have "the talk" with me about being gay, but he never did. I just assumed he didn't care because he's my parent and he has to love me through whatever. Little to my knowledge, he despised me.

Let's fast forward to recent times when I started to love and accept who I was as a person. I haven't seen my dad in over ten years after that last time he sent me back because "he couldn't handle my attitude." What did he expect from someone who barely knew him and had lacked any type of connection? I invited him to my home with my family because he claimed he wanted to get things right between us. I was with my fiance, who was of the same sex, a little over two years and he seemed as if it was okay. He joked and even went out in public with us. I thought everything was fine. I felt good about him this time. My fiancée had concerns that it was all a front because she had seen that same "look" in her own father's eyes before. I was so proud of her and everything we had accomplished together that I didn't even notice his negativity. He came to visit from Minnesota a few more times before I decided that it'd be the last time I ever saw him.

"Did you ever hear about the rose that grew from a crack in the concrete?" I never understood what Tupac was saying in this poem until recently. I used to be so scared to stick up for myself when it came to my parents, only because I was taught to respect my elders no matter what, but this is just one man I could not respect. My fiancée ended up being murdered in the summer of 2022. I hadn't talked to my dad since March of 2022 for other personal reasons. I ended up reaching out to him because I just felt like maybe I do need him in my life. After our conversation he did not hesitate to tell me that, "Maybe if she followed the 'book of God' she would still be here. You guys weren't living the way God wanted you to. You belong with a man, not a woman. It was a punishment." I lost it at this moment. I hung up on him and sent a text that said, "I'm sorry you feel the way you do, but I love who I love and cannot change that. I do not want to speak to you anymore after that comment because it hurt my feelings. For someone to say something so hateful like that after being around us and saying how you accept us, is heartbreaking. I hope you have a good life." He sent a text back saying, "I don't care. You're not my daughter anymore." I never thought I'd feel so relieved after saying that to him.

Equality isn't just needed for racism. Homosexuality is among us also, and the LGBT community suffers daily with the hatred and backlash we receive. In my opinion, if everyone minded their business the world would be a much happier place. Instead of worrying about who loves who, we should learn to love one another. My dad was cut off from my life after he made that comment to me. I don't have that parent-child love for him, so it isn't like it's a major loss. He can love me from a distance.

Cherie Maxwell

The Rose That Grew From Concrete

Try growing up in a place where there's no love, no safe space, no affection, or even no protection. Just on this lonely earth place without guidance, roads without destinations. You have homes without walls, homes with no structures, and homes without roofs — hearts with no love, and faces with no smiles. Try going through life alone without love and protection, but still find a way to grow when no one believes in you.

Growing up was difficult with no support at home while trying to figure out this thing called life. Being the only child who didn't have the same father as my other siblings, I was always on my own. Always feeling like I wasn't good enough — the feeling of being unworthy by the people that are supposed to care for you, love, and protect you. Always feeling like an outsider, no one to call on, no one to hear me cry.

Making my way on this journey looking for a higher calling within myself. Never giving up on me, loving me unapologetically, searching for the "man in the mirror," Michael Jackson said it best. Always feeling like I'm jogging in place, never really going nowhere. Working alone on this journey and it's the only option. Figuring out how to move without love and support is tough.

So here I am again, but this time on a different journey alone. A more promising journey where I can smell the roses, I can see the stars, everything is at arm's reach. Starting this chapter I never thought that I could make it through. As the smoke clears the view is beautiful, but yet still in a world all alone, no one to share with. Alone is uncomfortable but it makes you stronger. Could you imagine being a flower with no water, no food or no air to grow, no room to breathe?

Here I stand strong — alone yet filled with love and determination in the fight for my future. Never giving up on my quest to find that extra piece that fits my puzzle. Loving this new space, making it to the finish line with joy in my heart, my cup all the way filled, roads with a destination, faces with smiles, and hearts filled with love. The smoke is clear and I see the light at the end of the tunnel. Without air to grow, without air to breathe, without food to eat "I Am The Rose That Grew From Concrete."

Me Myself and I

Me Myself and I, I myself and me. Although I'm only one, sometimes I feel like three. Sometimes up and sometimes down, it feels though my best friend is always wearing a frown. Me myself and I, running free running wild. That's my best disguise, can't you tell?

So unhappy I could die, nothing changes so I've considered the try. I stopped and said to myself, this is the easy way out.

Why not challenge the world? I cry up a storm that throws my mind in a swirl. Then I looked in the mirror And the reflection said you got to love you. Because nothing comes easy. I have dreams of my own too And it's true, Straight to the sun we'll fly Me, Myself and I. Sometimes I feel as if I'm standing on a cliff but you can't let the wind blow, I must be happy for myself And for no one else.

I need someone to love me over time. I stumble through the darkness in my mind. I'm running through an hourglass out of time. Then I turned to the mirror And my reflection said, You got to love Because nothing never comes easy, I have dreams of my own too. And it's true, straight to the sun we'll fly Me Myself and I.

The theme of this poem is to prioritize myself and stay strong. Even though life might be hard, you gotta put yourself first. I cried so hard thinking things would get better. I even thought that dying was a way out, but life has changed for me. People that are going through things in life have to remember to stay strong because, like I said, "nothing never comes easy." That God is on your side, no matter what happens in life we can overcome. You have to believe in yourself that all things will come together. And dying is not the answer. This poem promotes change because it shows others that you don't have to take the easy way out. This poem shows others that it's okay to feel sad and go through tough times. But we still have to always "turn to the mirror" and love ourselves. Learning how to love yourself is so important. This is because sometimes you are gonna be your only support system at certain times in your life. So if you love yourself, then you will "fly" "straight to the sun" just like the poem says. Promoting the strength in loving yourself and not taking the easy way out is why this poem develops changes within others.

"Still I Rise" by Maya Angelou is a poem that also refers to the trials and tribulations that she had to overcome. Even though those times were hard, she was able to change her mindset, able to rise up and conquer all obstacles that came her way. "Did you want to see me broken? / Bowed head and lowered eyes? / Shoulders falling down like teardrops, / Weakened by my soulful cries?" (Angelou lines 16-19). Angelou may not have had help or a lot of encouraging individuals, but she did not allow them to affect her outcome. She did not allow anyone to take away her power and rose above all odds that were against her, like how I did in my poem.

Work Cited

Angelou, Maya. *The Complete Collected Poems of Maya Angelou*. Random House, 1994.

Ariel Santiago

Bloom

As i remember my identity and who i wanna be
It all started with Sylvia and Marsha P
Fighting for the right to live and be seen
If it weren't for the pioneers before me
I wouldn't have the right to be free
Blooming into the person i'm meant to be
Breaking the cage inside of me
As a caterpillar to a butterfly
I let my true colors shine
Picking up every piece of this life of mine.
Loving myself is what's truly divine.

"We have to be visible, we are not ashamed of who we are," are wise words spoken by trans activist Sylvia Rivera. I wrote this poem to express my journey as being a part of the trans community myself. The changes I've gone through, from how I look to how I'm treated, has affected me in many ways. Life as someone who identifies as a transwoman has been difficult. I may not look the part on the Zoom screen because of my fear of judgment but that doesn't mean I don't authentically live as myself outside of it. As I stated, "As a caterpillar to a butterfly," I was referencing my decision to change my gender. I've been transitioning since 2020 and the paths I've been on taught me so much about myself. Letting go and just expressing the person you are feels so freeing; it's been the best decision I've made.

This poem promotes change and shows how I bloomed as an individual, showing others to let your true self shine and be the best version of yourself you can be. This poem promotes change because I'm showing change within myself, but also sharing light as in how those I look up to took charge and gave me my spark to do what's right for me. As I stated in my poem, "It all started with Sylvia and Marsha P." What I was hinting towards was fighting for change in yourself and what's around you, to bring out what you truly feel like is right, just like how Marsha P. Johnson and Sylvia Rivera did back in their time with the Stonewall Riots and movements for the trans community.

Emily Nussbaum's "American Untouchable," also shows the fight for change and for what you believe is right. African American actor P. Jay Sidney, fought for African Americans to get equal jobs and roles as those that were lighter-skinned. "People today benefit from things that were sacrificed years ago," (Nussbaum par. 3), is a quote by Sidney's ex-wife, Carol Foster Sidney, that references what was sacrificed years ago is now accepted for those in my time. This provides change on how so many people before us gave up everything they had to fight for change and acceptance, the same way Johnson and Rivera fought as hard as Sidney did. I gained so much from this reading because it showed if I fight for myself and for my acceptance it'll happen. If Sidney didn't let anything stop him, then certainly I shouldn't stop embracing myself as I do now.

Work Cited

Nussbaum, Emily. "American Untouchable: the Actor who Fought to Integrate Early TV." *The New Yorker*, 30 Nov. 2015, www.newyorker.com/magazine/2015/12/07/american-untouchable.

Student Biographies

Mariah Bennett

I'm a woman, a mother, and an outgoing person. I love listening to music every day. It soothes me. I wake up every day loving the person I'm turning into. I'm going to be a future medical assistant. I love helping people in any way I can.

Ryan Bonilla

My name is Ryan Bonilla. I am an opportunist and an artist. I create my own music with my friends and want to have a lot of goals in my life completed by the time I'm 28. I shall have three cars and two jobs. I want to own my own business in barbering. I plan on helping kids who have a similar story as mine. I want to change millions of minds and help others reach their full potential.

Rosemary Bostwick

I am a daughter of two wonderful parents. I am a sister of two brothers and two sisters. (I am the middle child). I am a mother of five wonderful kids: three boys and two girls. As a mother, my life is 24/7 all about my family. I love to cook for my kids and create new meals that my family loves. I love taking pictures and capturing memories with my family. And in my very little spare time, I love to do crafts and I am teaching myself to sew. I love what I create, but most of all I love when others love what I can create for them. My crafting is my go-to, my self-therapy. I am a woman who is all about family because without family I wouldn't be me.

Martha Cruz

Hard to explain all of the things inside me. Hoping to God my lessons will guide me. There's so much good and a lot of bad, trying to avoid what makes me sad. My future is bright. I pick from within a dizzy life and hope my head won't spin. Never give up; it's not an option. You can chop me down, but never be surprised when I rise.

Constance Dickinson

I am a single Black woman who has two beautiful kids that I am proud of. I am a student and a hard-working woman with the potential of becoming a Medical Assistant. I enjoy teaching, helping people, traveling, and being around family. I am a Christian with great family morals. I am a person that enjoys life and what life has to offer. I am also a great cook and I was born and raised on a farm in the country. I am proud of all these things that make me me.

Luis Flores

The fear of leaving home at such a young age stuck with me
The fear of leaving my passing brother
The fear of a new language
The fear of what people thought of me
From then on I knew who I was
I wasn't going to let people bring me down
Pressured to become someone I wasn't
From then on I knew who I was
I always knew I wanted to do something with cars
I always knew I wanted to be a father
I didn't know I would become one this fast
Pressured to become someone I wasn't became what I was
Working at a young age to provide for my new family
I was thought to be a nobody
That's when I knew who I was again
That's when I started working not only for my family, but for me
I started working on what I loved
Working for the people that loved me

Leticia Garcia

I am a Mother, a Grandma, a hardworking single parent who always made sure my kids had everything they wanted and needed. I am my kids' superwoman 'cause no matter what happened in life I always made sure we were good. As a mother at such a young age, I had a lot of responsibilities, and one of my main concerns was to get my kids out of the neighborhood I was living in because, at the time, it was bad and every year was getting worse. So I got a full time job, and after working about a year, me and my kids' dad got our first apartment in a nice neighborhood. From then on, we made sure my kids went to a good school and had everything they needed, putting them in activities like basketball and football to keep them busy and occupied and they were safe to go outside and play. And everything I went through with my kids' dad and getting sick when I had my small stroke. And just not giving up no matter what came my way because I knew I was really the only one my kids had, and till this day I'm still the only one they have! And my kids are grown, 30 and 25, and I will do anything for them or help them in any way and they know that.

Mykayla Hall

I'm Mykayla. I'm a woman. I love being a black african american woman
I'm a mother of one. lol yes one 'n done
what makes me me is my personality, I'm open and very loving and caring to others
it's all smiles and laughter when I'm in the room
I'm a student with a path to complete, all my goals very focused
I'm your future business owner
aunt of one who I claim as my lil old cute broke bestfriend
I'm little beautiful ole me
Grateful and thankful for the person I am and the person I'm becoming

Tina Hannah

My mother had three daughters who also became mothers,
I am a mother of seven and also a grandmother of one,
I share my light on each and every one of them, even though I am the
Youngest, they treat me as if I'm the oldest, it gets hard sometimes but I wear the crown
As it was made for my head, I never let it tilt, I just go with the flow
Because I know I'm the one who gon' let my family grow.

Ebony Hardnett

I am a beautiful black woman
A woman that's not great
I am a mother
A blended family mother of eleven
I am a queen
A queen with plenty dreams and vision
I am not an artist
A teacher, I am, that can say I honestly love those kids
I am a woman that loves everyone
I am a woman that still has plenty faith
I am a woman that has plans
I am a woman that shows someone can
I am a woman that knows everyone can stand together again
I am Ebony Hardnett
I am the woman that says THE END

Nicholas Henderson

Who am I? I am a cool, down to earth person with a big imagination
I am an artist that loves to create and express my thoughts through pictures and art.
I am a musician that records my feelings over dope instrumentals.
I am an awesome dad that loves and enjoys his children no matter what life throws at him.
I am a loving and romantic husband that goes above and beyond to keep my spouse happy.
I am a big brother that you can call on whenever you need advice or someone to vent to.
I am a cool son that honors and respects my parents through all the rough times.
I am a hard worker that's going to get the job done by any means.
I am a friend who you can have fun with and also depend on.
I am a go-getter, meaning I'm a dream chaser that won't stop till I achieve.
I am a soon-to-be HSED graduate with intentions to attend college.
I am just me, Nicholas Henderson.

Filo Hernandez

Gentleman as far as my father can throw
me, Distracted like any other, not needing
but would like, Extraordinary just
like old and new, Father and husband
is what I do.

Otis Jackson

Hello, my name is Otis and out of four siblings, I'm the oldest. I consider myself a good father, a down-to-earth person, as well as an excellent barber. An old man blessed with the gift of gab and when not on the mic, you can catch me on the river fishing for slabs. Energetic on point when hiking these trails, but, at the same time, reciting lyrics from off of the head.

Jenevi Lal Par

Celebrate my Identity:
I am a woman. Strong and proud.
I am a mother. With love and kindness in my heart, you'll find.
I am a student. Ready to learn and grow to chase my dream.
I am a foodie. I like to taste all the food and don't have a favorite.

I am a Christian. Finding solace in faith and spreading kindness.
I am a movie lover. I enjoy watching movies or series, transporting myself to different worlds through the screen. I appreciate the beauty in life.
I celebrate the woman I am, unapologetic in my existence. I celebrate the mother I am, guiding my children with love and affection. I celebrate the student I am, seeking knowledge and learning. I celebrate the foodie I am, all food tastes good to me. I celebrate the Christian I am, finding strength and compassion in my beliefs. I celebrate the movie lover I am, transporting myself to different worlds through the screen.

Katravia Lee

I'm a very spiritual person; I can feel energy. I'm a mother of three beautiful little girls, whom I spend most of my days with. I'm here to pave a way for my children and myself. I'm a leader; I'm leading the way so my children can follow in my footsteps, achieving goals and prospering in the best way. I love hard. I still love the ones who scarred my heart, but from a distance. It took a while for me to finally understand my purpose, and it may take you a while to understand me and where I've been in life. I love the woman I'm becoming, I'm very understanding and generous, but I sense when my generosity is taken for granted. I love writing, and I will become a book writer. Coloring and drawing are a hobby that I do a lot with my kids. I'm a cook, an upcoming chef. I love making all my food from scratch. My favorite thing to cook is hibachi, a Japanese dish. I love music. Music calms my nerves. I am who I am. I am me.

Dombanee Lincoln

I am Dombanee
I am a Mother
I am beautiful
I am strong
I am prideful
I am stubborn
I am the glue that holds my family together
I am a fighter even with tears in my eyes
I am a kind and caring person
I am a person who loves to work

Clarissa Lugardo

A proud Puerto Rican and Mexican
I was raised to be a woman of independence

A current mother of three
Being a boy mom is not for the weak

At 30 years of life
I'm far from the finish line

Taught to have it all together
But this time feels like forever

Cherishing all the goods
Enjoying everything down to the foods

Pushing myself each day to be my best
I'm no longer settling for less

No matter what obstacles
I am a cardinal

Waking up everyday with a new song
My playlist could do no wrong

Unique to be me
Like a creative art piece

I don't need no one else
I am my own militia

Never will I be labeled a victim
Because my name is Clarissa.

Kenbri Lynn

I'm from Milwaukee where most days seem grey and winter is like the whole
year. I'm from I pray to keep you from the pains that will surely come, with a
hint of Kerri Brown. I am from a fear of insects; they gross me out. I am going
to start college and be the best I can for my firstborn.

Cherie Maxwell

My name is Cherie Maxwell. I am a highly motivated individual who loves
working for the people. I am a certified CBRF caregiver who specializes in as-
sisting the elderly. I also have experience in childcare as a Lead Teacher.

Haitham Mohammad

I'm from Jerusalem
where there's no traffic law
and people drive from age 12
and race to get to the other lane.

I'm from, Life is a Highway.
"Life's like a road that you travel on
when one day here and the next day
gone. Sometimes you bend, sometimes you stand,
sometimes you turn your back to the wind."

I'm from a fear of authoritarian government,
it freaks me out.

I am going on a vacation.

Dechante Nelson

Although I don't wear it on my sleeve,
My heart is a rainbow.
I get nervous around beautiful women who are just eating a sandwich in a
coffee shop.
I feel butterflies whenever "she" walks past because I can smell us dancing in
the field of roses.
The thorns getting stuck in my foot is similar to the pain in my chest when she
leaves and I can no longer catch my breath.
I am a lesbian.
"Mommy, mommy, can I have this?" rings through my ears even when they
aren't around.
Long days at the park.
Picnics are our favorite.
We play 'I Spy' to pass the time when we're in the car.
Each one has a little bit of my personality.
It's creepy but I dig it.
I am a mother.

Jasmine Northern

I'm a woman, a mother, and a Christian person. I'm here as God's gift — blos-
soms of flowers in the air. Celebrating life and completion of graduation, another step for the future. I love listening to soft and mellow music as I write my

poetry while the wind blows. I'm a beautiful courageous black queen going for what I deserve and desire in life. Worthy of overcoming all my obstacles and standing up for what I believe in. I am Jasmine Northern.

Enid Ortiz

I am an independent woman, a woman who has big dreams and inspires me to be more in this life. I am also a mother who loves her children, a mother who goes above and beyond for them and is their example to grow and be independent young women.

Shemar Parkes

I'm a woman, a mother, and a spiritual person.
I'm here to celebrate being me.
There is so much I can't explain.
I'm an open book.
It probably will take you a few
or couple of years to understand who I am.
I love everyone around me, even the one that wishes death upon me.
I have no hate inside my heart.
Wake up every day loving who I am.
I'm an artist, and I love painting, art, crafting, and songwriting.
I'm a music lover and food lover.
Eating jerk chicken, fried fish, and seafood is everything to me.
Where I'm from, music and food are really big.
The type of music I grew up listening to in Jamaica was Bob Marley.

Kimberly Ramsey

I am a mother, a woman, strong-headed, hard-working, and a stubborn person. I have anxiety and depression and I don't like being around people. I isolate myself a lot. Most people I meet say I'm a pretty cool person when you get to know me, but I'm very observant and picky about who I let into my life because I have been hurt. Who I am is Mommy! My kids call me. I really don't know myself outside of that and I'm okay with that. Everything I do is for our future. I am a first-time traditional student, who will graduate in a few years as a registered nurse. What made me is my fears, struggles, children, and my past experiences. I overcame the obstacles. I'm one step closer to success.

Xiomary Lee Rivera

As a social leader, Xiomarylee excels in teaching others with experience in management and training. She holds a conventional frame of mind, following set procedures and routines within the workplace. Professionally, she brings an innovative point of view to companies.

Vincente Rodriguez
This is me
Cooking is my newest passion, I love it.
Carne asada, ribs, steak,
I love cooking different meats.
I spend most free time gaming,
If not I'm with my boys playing.
I am a father of two beautiful boys,
Seeing them growing up makes me happy.
I love to play and watch soccer,
I am an only son of a Mexican mother,
Who taught me the ways of life.
I am me because of her, and my kids.
Aspiring to be a mechanic,
My job now is one step closer to my dream.

Jason Sanchez
I am a gay Latin American male. I'm an uncle of six. I'm a very loud person in a good way. Being such a free spirited person can get you far. I'm such a lover and I'm always interested in the next thing. I've always been so open to experiencing new things! Every day I wake up and the first thing I do to get my day going is play some music! There's so much to learn about me but that's the fun part about it! Traveling and experiencing different cultures makes me feel so alive. The tingly sensation when being miles in the sky. My culture itself has so many things to show. I grew up listening to all the good old school Spanish music and eating tons of fresh grown food, from fresh fruits grown out back to the freshly caught seafood.

Ariel Santiago
My Truth
Neither he or him just she and they
The shoulder you can lay your head on any day
Calm as my island's palm trees when i sway
Kpop music is what i love to play
My confidence you just can't take away
Whether glammed up or bareface

The beauty i have inside you can't replace
No more hiding in fear
Living freely as me takes courage my dear

Regina M. Scott
I'm a mother, a teacher, a hero, a caregiver, a leader, and most of all I am a woman. I'm a mother of three grown beautiful daughters. They are like a ray of sunshine, they brighten my day whenever I see or talk to them. I'm a teacher. I love teaching my K3s, the most colorful bunch of children, like a rainbow. I love watching them grow as the days pass us by. I'm a hero. I'm told every day by my students, "You are the best teacher and I want to be like you when I grow up." I'm a caregiver. I give my students the best of all. I treat them differently depending on their personalities. Some need more love, the others like flowers they grow every day with the love I give them. I'm a leader. I led my students in a positive direction, especially when they aren't having a good day. And most of all I am a woman. I love being celebrated on Mother's Day and my birthday because, first I share my birthday with my baby girl (she's 20 years old now), and second I have the best daughters. They showed me I did a very good job raising them.

Alaiah Outlaw Turner
Who Am I?
I identify as many names
A mother of which I have four kids
Even though I am a mother I am still
A child that came from my mother
    But wait that's not all
I can sing like a bird and type
Fast as a typewriter
Silly do you think that's all?
I'm also someone's sister,
A sister of three others you see,
I am the oldest one so not only am
I just a person to all of these people
I am a provider, protector, and just recently I became a wife!!!
I have so many names and all of this is what my
Identity is . . . What defines your identity?

Angie Rosales Vazquez
I am a mother and needed by two small children,

I'm the doctor, I'm the healer, I am needed.
I'm a rebel and enjoy taking a risk, living life on the edge.
  Can anyone control me, when will I submit?
I can smile in a crowd and laugh with the best,
But I'm most comfortable when the party's over.
  Who am I? I am a loner.
I don't live for myself, I live for my kids
  What happens when they grow up and
No longer need me to be the one . . . who am I?
  I AM NO ONE

Kevin Vazquez

My name is Kevin, and I'm 21 years old. I work at Walmart and I enjoy playing video games on my off days. I have a total of nine siblings! I'm working towards furthering my learning constantly.

Stephanie Vazquez

I am a woman. I'm a proud daughter of Mexican parents. I am the middle child out of seven children and also the middle sister out of five. I am a good sister and friend. I'm a good auntie. I became an aunt before a mom. I became a mom at the age of 25 and had a handsome little boy. I will be the 2nd generation to graduate along with one of my sisters that is attending the same school program as me and it makes me feel happy because it feels as if we were back in high school. I am engaged and hopefully after I graduate and complete school, I can go ahead with what I have planned to do. We can seal our commitment.

Yoana Vazquez

I am a woman that is 26 years old
I am a happy wife
I am a mom of four kids
I am a great and kind aunt
I love to eat ice cream
I love to eat fruit, my favorite is cherries

Monika Williams

I am a woman and a mother of four beautiful children: two boys and two girls. I love food. My favorite is chicken and pizza. I also love Chinese food. I pretty much love food of any kind as long as it's good. Most of the time I'm cooking, I'm trying something new. TV is one of my favorite things to watch. I like *The*

Walking Dead, All American, The Chi, and more. I love baking sweets: cookies, cakes, and pies. I braid hair. I do all kinds of braids: freestyle braids, box braids, and feed-in braids.

Kathryn Yang
I'm from Eau Claire
where it's a blink in my mind.
Now, living in Milwaukee for 10 years.

I'm from "turn the lights on
every night, I rush to my bed
with hopes that maybe I'll get
a chance to see you when I close
my eyes."

I am from a fear
of not overcoming my challenges
to be successful.

I am going to strive
to see the best of me
at all times.

Acknowledgements

About Literacy Services of Wisconsin

The writing and artwork featured in this collection were created through coursework at Literacy Services of Wisconsin. Literacy Services of Wisconsin partners with motivated adults to provide access to quality basic education and skills training so they can improve their lives, enrich their families, and strengthen our community.

Enroll: If you are interested in becoming a student, please call (414) 344-5878. You can also find more information in the enroll section of our website. Volunteer: If you are interested in becoming a tutor, or would like to provide other volunteer support, please email volunteer@literacyservices.org or call (414) 344-5878. You can also find more information in the volunteer section of our website. For additional information about Literacy Services of Wisconsin, please call (414) 344-5878.

About The Teaching Press at UW-Green Bay

This book was designed, copyedited, proofread, and prepared for press by the undergraduate intern team at The Teaching Press at UW-Green Bay. Emily Heling was the Book Designer. Autumn Johnson was the Chief Copyeditor. Interns on this project included T. Cottrell, Alex Guerrero, Samantha Landvick, Cole Murray, Dylan Nessman, Madeline Perry, Ezra Poulter, Charlotte Silverwood, Abby Wall, and Grace Zander. Rachel Mendez was the Press Manager who championed this project. The Teaching Press is directed by Dr. Rebecca Meacham.

The Teaching Press is a student-managed printing house and publisher at the University of Wisconsin-Green Bay. For our undergraduates, we offer hands-on learning and career preparation through transferable skills in writing, budgeting, editing, marketing, project management, workflow, and book design. For our authors, we welcome storytellers from all backgrounds, and we showcase stories from the Northeast Wisconsin region. For our communities, we connect bookmaking technologies with educators, K-12 students, organizations, and businesses.

uwgb.edu/teaching-press

www.ingramcontent.com/pod-product-compliance
Lightning Source LLC
Chambersburg PA
CBHW080755120626

46557CB00006B/1285